Teachers College Studies in Education

ART

in the

COLLEGE PROGRAM *of*

GENERAL EDUCATION

ERNEST ZIEGFELD, Ed.D.

Bureau of Publications

TEACHERS COLLEGE · COLUMBIA UNIVERSITY

NEW YORK · 1953

PREFACE

As the area of general education has expanded, and as its philosophy and procedures have been developed, it has become increasingly important to investigate the implications of this point of view with respect to the various subject-matter fields. There are a number of important questions to be answered regarding the contributions which a given subject area can make to the total program, and the methods by which the more specific aims of a given area can best be achieved in harmony with the underlying purposes of general education. To meet the need for a comprehensive statement regarding the implications of a philosophy of general education for the college art program has been the primary reason for undertaking the study.

The present volume is divided into three parts. Part One is devoted to an investigation of general education—what it is, why it has assumed such importance in the contemporary educational scene, what factors are responsible for its present direction, and what purposes it aims to achieve. In Part Two, the discussion turns to the arts as an aspect of human living—the nature of art experience, its significance for the individual, and its role in social development. An integration of these two aspects of the

vii

problem is the purpose of Part Three, and it attempts to develop the implications of the first two parts as they have relevance to the college program of art instruction. The chief contribution which the study purports to make is neither in the philosophy of general education nor in the philosophy of art, but rather in bringing the ideas from these two fields together and in exploring their implications for the art program of the college.

I wish to express my deep appreciation to my major adviser, Professor Arthur R. Young, and to the other members of my doctoral committee, Professor Karl W. Bigelow and Professor Ralph R. Fields, for the valuable help which they have given me and without which this study could not have been completed.

E. Z.

CONTENTS

ART

in the

COLLEGE PROGRAM *of*
GENERAL EDUCATION

Part One

**A VIEW OF
GENERAL EDUCATION**

Chapter I

A DEFINITION OF GENERAL EDUCATION

During the past two decades there has developed in this country a marked and growing interest in the area of general education. The increasing complexity and diversity of our American culture have forced the attention of educators to the extreme necessity for a type of education which will lead to more integrated patterns of group and individual living. The ideas which are basic to the concept of general education are not new or in any sense counter to our educational tradition. Eurich[1] has pointed out that our schools have always, to a greater or lesser degree, been concerned with general education —that the emphasis on the three R's which characterized our earliest grade schools and the traditional emphasis on citizenship training both represent efforts to provide youth with the means for more effective social interaction and responsible participation in a democratic society. The developments of the past few

[1] Alvin C. Eurich, "A Renewed Emphasis upon General Education," *General Education in the American College*, Thirty-eighth Yearbook of the National Society for the Study of Education, Part II (Bloomington: Public School Publishing Co., 1939), p. 3.

3

years, therefore, represent an increased emphasis on a historically established aspect of democratic education. As interest in the area has increased, there has been an intensive exploration of the nature of general education—the ends toward which it is directed and the means by which they may be most fully realized.

Considerable variation may be discovered in the more specific aims of general education which have been defined by various students of the subject. Basically, however, there is rather wide agreement as to the areas of human living which are the primary concern of general education. However diverse the specific ends and the means may be, they are uniformly concerned with the individual as a social being living and interacting within a cultural environment. The ultimate purpose of general education, stated so broadly as to allow no dissent, is to improve the quality of social interaction within our democratic society and thereby achieve a higher level of integration in group and individual living. The Report of the Harvard Committee defines general education as "that part of a student's whole education which looks first of all to his life as a responsible human being and as a citizen . . ." as opposed to special education "which looks to the student's competence in some occupation." [2] McGrath defines it as "that which prepares the young for the common life of their time and their kind." [3] The Report of the President's Commission on Higher Education refers to "those phases of nonspecialized and nonvocational learning which should be the common experience of all educated men and women." [4] Hutchins has commented as follows with respect to general education:

Everybody cannot be a specialist in every field. He must therefore be cut off from every field but his own unless he has the same basic education that other specialists have. This means more than having the same language and the same general interest in advanc-

[2] Harvard University Committee, *General Education in a Free Society* (Cambridge: Harvard University Press, 1946), p. 51.
[3] Earl J. McGrath and others, *Toward General Education* (New York: The Macmillan Company, 1948), pp. 8–9.
[4] The President's Commission on Higher Education, *Higher Education in American Democracy* (New York: Harper and Brothers, 1948), I, p. 49.

ing knowledge. It means having a common stock of fundamental ideas.[5]

There is apparent in these definitions a wide area of agreement in the sense that they are all primarily concerned with the individual as a member of society. The Harvard Report emphasizes the factor of responsible behavior as a citizen; McGrath speaks of preparation for the common life; the President's Commission frames its definition in terms of common experiences; and Hutchins refers to a common stock of fundamental ideas. All of them represent a move away from the intensive specialization and segmentation which have characterized much of American education during the years of its rapid growth and expansion. By contrast they are concerned with the development of human beings capable of a full and satisfying individual life and a high order of integration with their social and cultural environment. In amplifying the definition given above, McGrath says the following:

Not concerned with the esoteric and highly specialized knowledge of the scholar, general education includes neither the factual minutiae of investigations at the frontiers of knowledge nor the cultivation of the specialist's abilities and habits of mind. Without decrying professional education, research, or advanced specialized study, protagonists of general education maintain rather that these activities, laudable in themselves, should not prevent high schools and colleges from discharging their first responsibility—teaching young people how to live.[6]

General education, therefore, represents a redirection away from intensive subject-matter specialization and narrow vocational interests in favor of a greater emphasis on human and social values. It seeks to provide a rich context of individual and group living into which the achievements of the specialist may be more meaningfully integrated in terms of their significance for the life of our time.

It is apparent from this discussion that general education may be thought of in terms of two major aspects. The first of these

---

[5] Robert M. Hutchins, *The Higher Learning in America* (New Haven: Yale University Press, 1936), p. 59.
[6] McGrath and others, *op. cit.*, p. 10.

has to do with the development of those attitudes and understandings which will contribute to the unification and integration of our social life. Butts[7] has pointed out how the American
concept of democracy, during the period of rapid industrial expansion and the growth of the capitalist economy, came to be
defined primarily in terms of a rugged individualism whereby
the rights of the individual to pursue his own goals in his own
way greatly overshadowed his obligations to his fellow man.
Carried to its logical conclusion this philosophy leads to a society
in which "dog eats dog" and a group must be defined at its
lowest level as merely a collection of individuals. At a higher
level a group may be thought of as a unit composed of individuals bound together by certain broad purposes which provide
a flexible and dynamic field for the emergence and realization
of individual goals. It is this area of common purposes which
constitutes one of the major aspects of general education.

In discussing this aspect of general education, the President's
Commission has this to say:

General education should give to the student the values, attitudes,
knowledge, and skills that will equip him to live rightly and well
in a free society. It should enable him to identify, interpret, select,
and build into his own life those components of his cultural heritage
that contribute richly to understanding and appreciation of the
world in which he lives. It should therefore embrace ethical values,
scientific generalizations, and aesthetic conceptions, as well as an
understanding of the purposes and character of the political, economic, and social institutions that men have devised.[8]

It is important to note in the above quotation that the student
is to be equipped to live in a *free* society. This has far-reaching
implications for the way in which general education is conceived. Merely to speak of preparation for the common life or
of common experiences, unless such expressions are understood
to lie within a context of democratic living, may be most mis-
leading. The crux of the question lies not so much in whether
individuals will have common educational experiences, but
rather in the kind of behavior which will result from the ex-

[7] R. Freeman Butts, *The College Charts Its Course* (New York: McGraw-
Hill Book Co., 1939), p. 257.
[8] President's Commission, *op. cit.*, p. 49.

periences that are provided. The ideal of a totalitarian society is to give its citizens common experiences which will prepare them for life in their society, but the aim in this case is the suppression of free, spontaneous behavior and the cultivation of fixed patterns of response in terms of fixed and predetermined social ends. By contrast, the aim of education in a democratic society is to cultivate in the individual the desire and the capacity to relate himself spontaneously and creatively to his environment.[9]

The experiences which constitute any educational process, therefore, are to be regarded as means rather than ends; the behavior patterns which students build out of their educative experiences must be our primary concern. It thus appears that to define general education in terms of common experiences is to misplace the emphasis and to overlook the primary importance of behavior as the ultimate aim of education.

There is, in all probability, a rather large body of experience which should be shared by all members of a democratic society. But to define general education in terms of common experience presents several difficulties in addition to the one already mentioned. For one thing, similar behavior may result from many kinds of experience. For example, we may state as one of the purposes of general education the development of a respect for the rights of others. Such a respect may grow out of experiences in a student organization; a study of the works of Voltaire may be another way to achieve the same end; or this attitude may be strengthened through experience in social service work in an underprivileged neighborhood. How can it be determined, except in terms of the specific situation, which of these experiences will most effectively lead to the desired outcome? Defining general education in terms of common experiences poses the almost insuperable problem of making general statements about decisions which are contingent upon specific situations.

A third difficulty with such a definition is its implication that this body of common experiences defines the limits of general education. If our aim is to develop to the fullest each individual's

[9] See Erich Fromm, *Escape from Freedom* (New York: Rinehart & Co., 1941), ix+305 pp.

capacity "to live rightly and well in a free society," then such a definition is obviously inadequate. The same may be said of Hutchins's definition of general education as a common stock of fundamental ideas. This introduces the second major aspect of general education—that part which is concerned with equipping the student to live a rich individual life. Eurich has stated, as one of three propositions upon which a democratic concept of education is based, that "Each individual, while in constant and essential relationship to the society in which he lives, has a unique value." [10] The idea of democratic group action is based on the principle of variety in unity; it is the uniqueness of each individual's contribution to the group that gives richness and vitality to the life of the group. This means that the democratic community will prosper and flourish only to the extent that each member has the opportunity to develop his own unique capabilities. It becomes clear, therefore, that general education is in no sense uniform education—that it must be committed to the development of individual capacities and interests and to the meeting of individual needs at the same time that it provides the necessary social orientation for effective group participation.

The line between general education and special education thus appears to be somewhat blurred and indistinct. Development of individual interests and capacities does certainly take us into the realm of special education; indeed it is the particular province of special education. The distinction between the two types of education is well summarized in the definition quoted above from the Report of the Harvard Committee. General education is concerned with the individual "as a responsible human being and as a citizen"; special education "looks to the student's competence in some occupation." General education is thus concerned with the entire extra-vocational life of the student; we may go even further and say that it includes concern with those aspects of his vocational life which have to do with his own well-being and his ordinary relationships with his fellow men. It is directed toward making of him an intelligent, useful, and happy citizen.

It is true that the division suggested here between the two

[10] Eurich, *op. cit.,* p. 10.

kinds of education is still a hazy one, but it is so of necessity. Indeed, in any dynamic concept of life and education there can be no clear-cut division for, as Eurich has pointed out, "The entire range of the behavior of an individual involves interaction with other personalities." [11] This is not to say that there is not a distinct and very real difference between general education and special education but rather that the intricate and complex relationship which they bear to each other makes a sharp separation impossible.

In conclusion, then, we may define general education as that part of a student's total education which is primarily concerned with his life as a unique member of the social group. It seeks to foster within the student the development of behavior patterns which are conducive to a rich and satisfying individual life so oriented that it will be consistent with, and make a positive contribution to, the building and the realization of democratic goals. It is to be distinguished on the one hand from special education and on the other hand from uniform education. It is related to special education in that it provides a broader individual and social context within which the student may pursue his more highly specialized and vocational interests. At the same time it is committed to the meeting of individual needs and to the development of individual capacities and interests to the end that each individual, through a full realization of his own potentialities as a human being, can make a maximum contribution to the common good.

[11] *Loc. cit.*

Chapter II

FACTORS INFLUENCING THE GROWTH OF
THE GENERAL EDUCATION MOVEMENT

Any culture, whatever its philosophic basis and its social ideology, must, if it is to maintain itself, be concerned with general education. The relationship which the individual bears to the social group, whether it be fluid and dynamic or rigidly controlled, cannot be left to mere chance. A society *is* a society only to the extent that its members are bound together by a common heritage and common aspirations. The heritage is there —a pre-existent fact, so to speak—to be interpreted and drawn upon according to the lights of the particular social ideology. The process by which the aspirations of a people are evolved is enormously complex and it must be recognized at the outset that formal education is only one of many factors involved. It must further be recognized that education, at the same time that it is contributing to the building of aspirations and ideals, is also reflecting the ideals of the society in which it is operating. Therefore any meaningful discussion of general education must be carried on in terms of a particular culture or a particular social ideology. The present discussion will undertake to look at those factors in our American culture which have been responsible for the renewed emphasis on general education and for the direction which this emphasis has taken.

THE DEMOCRATIC PHILOSOPHY

In any discussion of American education, it is necessary first to examine the social philosophy upon which our culture is founded for, as the President's Commission has stated, "An educational system finds its guiding principles and ultimate goals in the aims and philosophy of the social order in which it functions."[1] Education in the American culture is committed to a democratic philosophy and it is within a context of democratic principles that it must operate. Therefore, in order to understand the background against which general education in this country has developed, it is necessary first to examine some of the concepts which are fundamental to the democratic way of life.

MAXIMUM GROWTH AND DEVELOPMENT
OF EVERY INDIVIDUAL

The basic principle of the democratic philosophy is the belief in the pre-eminent worth of the individual, the idea that, as Kilpatrick has stated it, "Each person is to be treated always as an *end* and never merely as a *means*. In this ethical respect," he continues, "all men are to stand equal."[2] The democratic state exists for the benefit of its members and, by its very nature, has strength and vitality only to the extent that its members have grown strong through the fulfillment of their individual capacities. The ideal toward which a democratic people strive is that condition of interaction in which each individual in the full realization of his own unique potentialities thereby makes his greatest

[1] The President's Commission on Higher Education, *Higher Education in American Democracy* (New York: Harper and Brothers, 1948), I, p. 5.

[2] William H. Kilpatrick, "Philosophy of Education from the Experimentalist Outlook," *Philosophies of Education*, Forty-first Yearbook of the National Society for the Study of Education, Part I (Chicago: The Society, 1942), p. 54.

contribution to the life of the group; and by the process of interaction his own life is further enriched by the greater vitality of
the group life to which he has contributed. Thus, to liberate the
potentialities of every individual is, at one and the same time,
the central purpose of a democratic society and its only means
for survival and growth.

The interactive process by which this takes place has been
summarized by Dix as follows:

A major defense of the individual against the increasing pressures
of . . . social life . . . lies in his capacity increasingly to cultivate
areas of living which have most immediate and rewarding effects
upon what might be called his internal sense of self. He cannot
withdraw from social life and remain healthy. He can increasingly
learn how to expand his inner life by means of those aspects of the
culture most appropriate to his temperament and tastes. The inter-
operation of these intimate personal factors with their appropriate
cultural opportunities will contribute to a sense of personal integration and to the long-time meaningfulness of his own life, while at
the same time his personal enrichment will contribute to the social
life in which he engages.[3]

This concept of individual growth in a democratic society
carries a twofold implication for education. First, it is necessary
to provide for and encourage the continuous growth of every
individual to the end that he may lead a richly satisfying personal life—a life which will make possible the full realization of
his "internal sense of self." As Hook has said, "There must be
some private altars in a public world where the human spirit can
refresh itself." [4]

There is, of course, always the danger that too great an emphasis on the private world of the individual will lead to attitudes
and patterns of behavior which are antisocial. This brings us to
the second point, which has to do with developing in the individual a sense of selfhood—a picture of himself as a responsible
human being in constant interaction with his environment. This
aspect of the democratic philosophy will be more fully dealt

[3] Lester Dix, *A Charter for Progressive Education* (New York: Bureau of
Publications, Teachers College, Columbia University, 1939), p. 38.
[4] Sidney Hook, *Education for Modern Man* (New York: Dial Press, 1946),
p. 13.

with in the following section but it seems important to note here that it is, in a very real sense, a part of the personal growth of every individual to develop that sense of integrity and responsibility which is essential for worthy social living.

One further point should be made with respect to this concept of individual growth and development. This is a goal which is in a continuous state of being realized for growth is a continuous process. To speak of maximum growth is in no sense meant to imply the attainment of a fixed goal beyond which the individual has no need nor opportunity to move. Rather growth is conceived as a dynamic process in which the attainment of each goal points the direction to new ones. By maximum growth is meant the fullest realization of potentialities which is possible at any given time in the light of both internal and external conditions. Education—formal education, that is—is not to be thought of, therefore, as the means whereby the student's growth is brought to completion. It is concerned, instead, with fostering the capacity and the desire for a kind of living which is itself a process of continual growth and development.

SOCIAL RESPONSIBILITY OF EVERY INDIVIDUAL

While it is true that the democratic society is devoted first and foremost to fostering freedom of the individual, it is equally true that, as the Report of the Harvard Committee has stated, "Democracy is a *community* of free men." "We are apt sometimes," the Report continues, "to stress freedom—the power of individual choice and the right to think for oneself—without taking sufficient account of the obligation to cooperate with our fellow men; democracy must represent an adjustment between the values of freedom and social living." [5] The right of freedom carries with it the responsibility for helping to build and maintain that kind of society in which all men have equal freedom. Indeed, as Fromm has shown, freedom *from* the restraints of a limiting physical and social environment may, by itself, be unendurable and lead the individual to escape into the security of authoritarian rule. Freedom is fully realized only when it is "a

[5] Harvard University Committee, *General Education in a Free Society* (Cambridge: Harvard University Press, 1946), p. 76.

state of positive freedom in which the individual exists as an independent self and yet is not isolated but united with the world, with other men, and nature. . . ." [6]

This carries several implications which, although they are closely interrelated, may, for greater clarity and convenience, be discussed separately. In the first place, it means that personal goals must be set with reference to the interests of the community. Freedom to do exactly as one wishes without reference to the welfare of others can result only in chaos. At the very least, the interests of the individual must not run counter to those of the group. At the very best, the individual's feeling of identity with the group will be such that personal interests and group interests, rather than conflicting, will give vitality and meaning each to the other. It is at the lowest level, and only at this level, that the enforcement of laws can be effective. Society can restrain a man from performing acts which do harm to the group, but it cannot legislate a sense of responsibility or the will to cooperate. Successful democratic living, therefore, is largely dependent upon personal choice which is guided by the individual's sense of loyalty and responsibility to the group.

A corollary of this concept of self-restraint in the interest of the group is the idea that the individual must have a sense of tolerance and respect for the interests, beliefs, and activities of others. These two ideas may, at first sight, appear to be contradictory; if every individual, in his concern for the group life, controls his activities in the interest of the group, then why should the occasion for tolerance ever arise? The answer seems to be that we are not living in a Utopian world. We live in a very real and imperfect world in which there are serious differences and conflicts in the beliefs men hold and the goals they deem desirable. The democratic society is always in the process of becoming; as old conflicts are resolved, new ones emerge. It is one of the great strengths of democracy that it can embrace such widely divergent beliefs and patterns of behavior. It is only when individuals and groups become intolerant of ideas which are in conflict with their own and lose the will to resolve differ-

[6] Erich Fromm, *Escape from Freedom* (New York: Rinehart and Co., 1941), p. 257.

ences by peaceful means that the structure of the democratic society is threatened.

A third aspect of the individual's responsibility to the group has to do with his loyalty to democratic beliefs and institutions. Democracy is not only *for* the people, it is also *of* the people and *by* the people. Its maintenance and growth are dependent upon the intelligent participation of all its citizens. Again, a contrast may be drawn between democratic and totalitarian societies. The latter exacts a blind and unquestioning loyalty, a complete submission to the edicts of the ruling group. Its citizens have the two alternatives of acceptance or revolution. Loyalty demands of them that they say, "My country is always right." The loyal member of a democratic society, on the other hand, may say, "My country, right or wrong!" and, having said it, will set about doing what he can to right the wrongs as he sees them.

This means, in effect, that democratic loyalty is a critical loyalty. But this alone is not enough, for the opinions which give rise to criticism must be informed opinions. Thus, the right to be critical carries with it several obligations: first, that criticism be of a constructive kind that looks toward a fuller realization of good for the group; second, that it be based on informed opinion; and third, that it be followed by intelligent and constructive action. What we know of human behavior seems to indicate that loyalty to a group results from a sense of participation in the activities of the group and of responsibility for its welfare. The most effective way, therefore, of eliciting loyalty from the citizens of a democratic society is to increase, both in range and in depth, their opportunities for active participation in controlling the affairs of society. The question of whether the individual's responsibility is a right or a privilege will then largely lose its significance; it will be an attitude engendered by his sense of worth with respect to the affairs of society.

COMMON UNDERSTANDINGS FOR THE ACHIEVEMENT
OF COMMON GOALS

In the preceding chapter, a group was defined as being, in the best sense, a unit composed of individuals bound together by certain broad purposes which provide a flexible and dynamic field for the emergence and realization of individual goals. In this connection, Dewey has noted that "There is honor among thieves, and a band of robbers has a common interest as respects its members." [7] The mere existence of a common purpose and common interests is not a sufficient criterion for evaluating the social worth of a group. "Any education given by a group," Dewey continues, "tends to socialize its members, but the quality and value of the socialization depends upon the habits and aims of the group." He suggests two criteria which may be applied to groups. The first one has to do with the number and variety of interests which are consciously shared. The second has to do with the extent and the freedom of intercourse with other groups. In amplifying his discussion, Dewey continues:

If we apply these considerations to, say, a criminal band, we find that the ties which consciously hold the members together are few in number, reducible almost to a common interest in plunder; and that they are of such a nature as to isolate the group from other groups with respect to give and take of the values of life. Hence, the education such a society gives is partial and distorted. If we take, on the other hand, the kind of family life which illustrates the standard, we find that there are material, intellectual, aesthetic interests in which all participate and that the progress of one member has worth for the experience of other members—it is readily communicable—and that the family is not an isolated whole, but enters intimately into relationships with business groups, with schools, with all the agencies of the culture, as well as with other similar groups, and that it plays a due part in the political organization and in return receives support from it. In short, there are many interests consciously communicated and shared; and there are varied and free points of contact with other modes of association.[8]

We shall concentrate here only on the first of these two criteria. Applied to a democratic society, it means that the quality of social living in that society is determined, in large part, by the extent to which there exists a wide area of common understanding and common goals. These common goals, furthermore, must be of such a nature that, through their achievement, they

---

[7] John Dewey, *Democracy and Education* (New York: The Macmillan Company, 1916), p. 95.
[8] *Ibid.*, pp. 96–97.

facilitate the realization of individual goals. In addition, the purposes of each member of the group must be mutually compatible with those of the other members. The performance of a group of musicians may serve to illustrate the point. The common goal which is held by all of them is to perform creditably, let us say, a Beethoven quartet. Within this framework each member has an individual role: he has a particular instrument and a particular score which he must play. His goal as an individual, therefore, is to play, as effectively as possible, his own score on his own instrument. But he is not playing as a soloist; he is playing as a member of a group and the effectiveness of his individual performance will depend, in large part, upon the extent to which all members have a common understanding of the music as a whole and gear their individual performances to it.

By themselves, therefore, common goals are not enough. Back of them must be an area of common understanding which is necessary to achieve a mutuality of effort. Returning to the musicians, let us assume, for a moment, that each of them, although sharing the common purpose of playing the quartet, has, because of his prior musical training, a completely different understanding of the work as a whole. Under such conditions the performance will be a poor one and the efforts of each player will be hampered, rather than helped, by the others.

Successful group living, then, depends upon shared purposes *and* shared understandings. Its richness and variety depend upon at least three factors. First, they will be determined by the variety of the goals which the group holds in common. If the four musicians share no other interest but to perform quartet music the significance of this group interest will be a relatively minor factor in the total life of any one of them. The second element is the degree of importance which the group goals possess for the individual. The common desire to perform quartet music will constitute a much stronger bond for four professional musicians who are deeply interested in music than for a group of adolescents who are being forced by their parents to take music lessons. The third factor is the degree to which a shared goal necessitates mutual and cooperative action for its achievement. Two thousand people may be assembled in an auditorium with the common purpose of seeing a motion picture; the realization of this purpose, however, demands no cooperative effort except that all members of the audience remain in their seats and refrain from making a disturbance. Thus the bond which holds the members of the audience together as a group is negligible.

It should perhaps be reiterated at this point that not all living is group living, that there are some aspects of an individual's life which he does not wish to share—indeed, which he cannot share —with his fellow men. It is inevitable that conflicts will sometimes arise between an individual's private world and his social world. The success with which he is able to resolve these conflicts is a measure of his own internal integration and his ability to relate himself to the environment in which he lives. With respect to the culture, the frequency and the depth of such conflicts is one of the measures of the diversity and flexibility which it possesses. The ideal toward which the democratic society strives is a condition in which individual and social goals are reciprocal in the sense that each is best realized as the other is realized.

MAXIMUM INTERACTION BETWEEN INDIVIDUALS
AND BETWEEN GROUPS

In the excerpt quoted above from Dewey's *Democracy and Education*, the second criterion for the evaluation of group living has to do with the extent and the freedom of contact with other groups. This concept may be examined with respect first, to the individual, second, to groups within the democratic society, and lastly, to the society as a whole.

In a rigidly structured authoritarian society, there are severe limits set upon the individual's freedom to move from one group to another or even to have free contact with groups other than his own. The stratification of classes and groups may have many different bases: social position, wealth, occupation, religious beliefs, political ideas, racial inheritance—these are some of the factors which have operated most frequently in our Western culture. The democratic concept of group formation proceeds from the idea that the purpose of any group is the improvement and enrichment of individual living. Therefore, the individual is attracted to, and associates himself with, those groups which give greatest promise of meeting his particular needs and interests and of challenging his capacities. As his needs and interests change, his group associations will change.

Closely related to this idea of mobility in group association is the idea of multiplicity and variety. The richness of an individual's life depends not only on the intensity of his interests but also on their number and their variety. It is important, therefore, that he should be able to associate simultaneously with many different groups representing a variety of interests.

This brings us to the heart of Dewey's discussion in which he compares the group life of a criminal band and a family unit, and which has application, here, to the relationship between groups in a democratic society. The interests and aims of the robber band are such as to eliminate mutually desirable contacts with other groups. The activities of the family, on the other hand, lead naturally and easily to associations with other groups which result in mutual gain. The generalization which these examples serve to illustrate is that just as the life of an individual is enriched through his associations with others so the activities of groups will gain in vitality and meaning as they allow for and encourage a free interrelationship with other groups.

There is always the danger that a discussion such as this may become so preoccupied with describing the ideal democratic society that it has little meaning with respect to the actual world in which we live. It is inevitable, especially in a society as varied as ours, that there will be groups, all proclaiming their devotion to the ideals of democracy and their interest in the common good, but still in direct conflict with respect to their specific goals and interests. This is not necessarily to be deplored; perfect agreement on all issues of importance among one hundred and fifty million Americans would be a most unhappy, and even dangerous, condition, for, as Follett has shown, conflict and disagreement provide the motivation for the discovery of new alternatives and new modes of behavior.

We can measure our progress by watching the nature of our conflicts. Social progress is in this respect like individual progress; we become spiritually more and more developed as our conflicts rise to higher levels. If a man should tell you that his chief daily conflict with himself is—Shall I steal or not steal?—you would know what to think of his state of development. As someone has said, "A man is known by the dilemmas he keeps." In the same way, one test of your business organization is not how many conflicts you have, for conflicts are the essence of life, but *what* are your conflicts? And how do you deal with them? It is to be hoped that we shall not always have strikes, but it is equally to be hoped that we shall always have conflict, the kind which leads to invention, to the emergence of new values.[9]

Seen from this point of view, the great diversity which exists in this country is a potential source of vitality and growth. Conflict becomes disruptive and dangerous when it reaches the point where the only contacts between groups are aggressive ones and the will to resolve differences has been lost. When this will exists it provides a basis for the building of intergroup understanding.

This same criterion of free and multiple contacts may be applied to the democratic society as a whole. In the ancient world it was possible for culture groups to live in relative isolation from one another; contacts were infrequent because they were difficult to make and because each group was largely self-sufficient. Today we have no alternative to close association with other groups because we are faced with the undeniable fact of a world made up of closely interrelated cultures. The question, therefore, is not whether we shall have contact with other cultures but what the nature and intent of such contacts will be.

In this respect, as well, we have no real alternative in the face of possible annihilation through atomic warfare. The President's Commission on Higher Education has said:

In a world in which technology is acting as a solvent of cultures, the historic concept of international relations—political, economic, and cultural—will have to be modified if contemporary civilization is to survive. No longer can peoples hope to build their security and the peace of the world on national strength and balance of power arrangements.

[9] Mary Parker Follett, *Dynamic Administration: The Collected Papers of Mary Parker Follett;* ed. by Henry C. Metcalf and L. Urwick (New York: Harper and Brothers, 1942), pp. 35–36.

The competitive principle, so long dominant in international relations, must give place, if nations are to survive, to principles of cooperation. . . .[10]

At this level also the concept of mutual gain through association is our guiding principle. In fact, it is at this level that the principle is most dramatically illustrated, for we must make the choice between mutual gain and mutual destruction. Democracy subscribes to the belief that through cooperative effort based on common understanding we can achieve a unified and peaceful world.

DIVISIVE INFLUENCES IN THE AMERICAN CULTURE

The foregoing section has presented a philosophy for democratic living which provides one of the mainsprings for the general education movement in this country. That the kind of living envisaged here has not been realized—or, at least, has been only partially realized—is all too evident. The most cursory glance at our civilization reveals enormous disparities between our present patterns and the kind of living which would represent an approximation of the democratic ideal. There are in our present culture a number of factors which have inhibited the growth of democratic forms, which have tended to divide rather than to unify, and which have led, not toward integration, but toward isolation of the individual from the social group and division and sharp conflict between groups.

It has already been stated that a system of education is guided in the formulation of its goals by the social philosophy of the group in which it is operating. Speaking metaphorically, it is just as important to know one's point of departure as it is to know one's destination; education is guided, not only by a social philosophy, but also by a realistic appraisal of the present state of affairs. It is the purpose of this section to review those factors in our culture which have engendered division and disunity and which, for this reason, have been responsible for the present emphasis on the integrative functions of general education.

[10] President's Commission, *op. cit.,* p. 15.

UNEVENNESS OF CHANGE

It is a commonplace that one of the chief characteristics of our age is the fact of rapid and profound change. It is equally true that there is a marked unevenness in the rate at which change has occurred in the various areas of our living. Within the past two centuries, science and technology have revolutionized the material facts of our existence, and as the material environment has been thus altered we have had no alternative but to accept and adapt ourselves to radically new patterns of living. At the same time, many areas of our thinking and behaving have exhibited a marked resistance to change. We are especially congenial to change in the physical sciences and technology, and we hail it as evidence of our national fertility and strength. But in many other areas of living, especially the social sciences and the arts, we tend to cling to "established" values. To complicate matters still further, we exhibit considerable ambivalence toward many of these "established" or traditional values, supporting them only if they do not conflict with the realities of our technological, materialistic culture. This ambivalence has led to the kind of contradictory assumptions which Lynd has enumerated in *Knowledge for What?* Typical of these contradictions are the following:

The family is our basic institution and the sacred core of our national life.
But: Business is our most important institution, and, since national welfare depends upon it, other institutions must conform to its needs.

Religion and "the finer things of life" are our ultimate values and the things all of us are really working for.
But: A man owes it to himself and to his family to make as much money as he can.

· · · · ·

Science is a fine thing in its place and our future depends upon it.
But: Science has no right to interfere with such things as business and our other fundamental institutions. The thing to do is to use science, but not to let it upset things.

Children are a blessing.
But: You should not have more children than you can afford.[11]

[11] Robert S. Lynd, *Knowledge for What? The Place of Social Science in American Culture* (Princeton: Princeton University Press, 1939), pp. 60–62.

The reasons for this decided unevenness in our willingness to accept or to institute change are extremely complex and it is beyond the scope of the present study to explore them. Lynd has pointed to what is perhaps the most important factor when he says, ". . . we exhibit marked hospitality to certain types of change—for instance in our technologies—while the strain of adjustment to these large and rapid changes makes us conservatively resistant to undergoing the tension of change at other points. . . ." [12]

The result is that as we resist the tension of change we open the door to deeper and more disruptive tensions between social groups and within individuals. The contradictory assumptions which are quoted above can easily be identified with different groups and institutions in our culture. For example, while social scientists endeavor to apply their findings to the operation of our economic life, business groups proclaim the validity, and even the sanctity, of a *laissez-faire* economy. It may be said, on the one hand, that the uneven rate of change in our cultural patterns is due to the influence of firmly established groups and institutions in our society. At the same time, the strength with which these institutions hold our loyalty is an indication and a reflection of the dual attitude which we, as individuals, have toward the phenomenon of change. The result, in any case, is disunity and conflict among social groups; for the individual it leads either to a blind compartmentalization of values or to inner conflict and frustration of a most disruptive nature.

FORMATION OF SUBGROUP LOYALTIES

While unevenness in the rate of change is one of the reasons for what Lynd has called "the deeply fissured surface of our American culture," it provides only a partial explanation. Even more serious than the rate of change is the enormous variation in the direction of change which is deemed desirable by different groups. Some of this variation, it is true, may be attributed to the disparity between traditional values and contemporary developments. But the lines which divide groups are drawn in many different directions and originate from a variety of

[12] *Ibid.*, p. 101.

sources. Individuals tend to be drawn together on the basis of common backgrounds, experiences, and interests; in a culture as complex and as varied as ours, the centers of interest around which group loyalties are formed are enormous in number and variety. This, in itself, is not a bad thing; as was indicated earlier, multiplicity and variety in group association is one of the strengths of a democratic society. But it is a strength only so long as there is a free association between groups which results in mutual benefit. As the aims and interests of groups diverge to the point where loyalty to group A carries with it hostility to group B, the result is disruption and division. The sources of intergroup conflict in our culture are much too numerous and complex to receive an extensive treatment here. It will be possible only to indicate, in a very general way, the major areas in which lines between groups have been most sharply drawn and the resulting conflicts have been most marked.

Probably the sharpest and the most pervasive conflicts in our culture arise out of economic differences. These differences are of several kinds. In the first place, there are enormous inequalities in the distribution of wealth. An analysis of federal income tax returns for the year 1946[13] shows that the average of the incomes reported was slightly over $2550, while the median was just over $2000. The following summary will give some idea of the range and concentration of wealth as reflected in the incomes reported for that year.

Nearly 11,000,000 of the returns, or 20.7 per cent of the total, reported incomes of less than $1000.

Over 26,000,000 of the returns, or 49.5 per cent of the total, reported incomes of less than $2000.

Over 39,000,000 of the returns, or 75.1 per cent of the total, reported incomes of less than $3000.

Somewhat over 3,000,000 returns, or 6.2 per cent of the total, reported incomes in excess of $5000.

Less than 1,000,000 of the returns, or 1.8 per cent of the total, reported incomes in excess of $10,000.

Less than 200,000 returns, or about .37 of one per cent of the total, reported incomes in excess of $25,000.

[13] Data taken from U. S. Bureau of the Census, *Statistical Abstract of the United States: 1949* (Washington: U. S. Government Printing Office, 1949), p. 339.

Further analysis shows that at the lower end of the scale about 21 per cent of the returns represented only 4.4 per cent of the total income reported. At the other extreme, 1.8 per cent of the returns accounted for better than 15 per cent of the total income reported. Making due allowance for the fact that these figures represent only a rough approximation of the total picture, they still reflect enormous inequalities in economic status.

Closely related to the fact of unequal distribution of wealth, but bearing a somewhat different emphasis, is the economic conflict between the owners and managers of productive enterprise and the workers. It is neither possible nor necessary to review here the evidences of strife between capital and labor. It is necessary only to note that it represents one of the deepest rifts in our national life; and there is no evidence that the tension is relaxing.

Another source of economic conflict has to do with differences which arise between groups as a result of their varying means of livelihood. The conflict between the farmer and the urban worker has a long history in our culture. The American Federation of Musicians has fought bitterly the inroads which have been made by the radio and phonograph industries on the employment of "live" performers. Members of the building trades unions offer strong opposition to any technological developments, such as prefabricated housing, which threaten to reduce their employment. The struggle is bitter because the maintenance of economic security seems to depend upon the complete elimination of any opposing interests.

Because economic security is one of the basic needs of living, it is easy to understand why the opposition is so strong between individuals of different economic levels and interests. Furthermore, it is not a discrete and separate area, for it deeply permeates and influences—indeed, in some cases, is basic to—many of the other areas of conflict within the culture.

A second point of strain within the culture, and one which is closely related to economic interests, is in the area of political ideologies. While it is true that there have always been many shades of political opinion in this country, it may be said that, by and large, the conflict centers in the opposition between liberal and conservative interests. In fact, in the present climate of recrimination and name-calling, it seems that the lines are being more sharply drawn and it becomes increasingly difficult for the individual to maintain an independent middle position.

It is true that it is always one of the conditions of conflict that as major issues are sharpened opposing groups tend to be forced into more extreme positions, and the individual must choose either to identify himself with the position of the group or to withdraw from the controversy entirely. In the contrast between political ideologies this condition is especially crucial because politics and government have such direct and widespread implications for all the major areas of our living. This means that the split between liberalism and conservatism represents a split with respect to practically all phases of our social and economic life.

By itself, the fact that political conflict has such widespread implications for all the areas of our living is sufficient to explain its disruptive effects. However, the present situation is further complicated by the increasing tendency to create political stereotypes. Once an individual has been identified as either a liberal or a conservative, even though the evidence may be most inconclusive, there is no hesitancy about predicting what his position will be with respect to all the major political issues of the day. It is true that people will generally exhibit a good deal of consistency in their positions with respect to such diverse issues as housing, civil rights, government control of business, education, and control of atomic energy. Still, each issue should be considered on its own merit, and the tendency to hew to a "party line" regardless of the merits of the particular case serves to deepen the conflict between opposing groups and contributes little to a constructive solution of the problems.

Another unfortunate aspect of this tendency to create stereotypes is the feeling of fear which it engenders in an individual whose opinions on any issue run counter to the interests of powerful groups. If he signs a petition demanding the outlawing of atomic warfare, he risks being labeled a pro-Communist, or even a Communist. When he supports legislation for the extension of medical benefits through government agencies, he is, at best, a Socialist. In an increasing number of cases, the individual places his professional and social life in jeopardy by an honest and open statement of his political convictions. The results of such a situation are personal fear and insecurity, secretiveness, and deceit.

A final aspect of our political life which has most serious consequences is the political apathy of a large segment of our population. Figures published by the American Institute of Public Opinion[14] show that in 1940, the most recent year for which complete data are available, only 63 per cent of the total voting population participated in the national election; and for local and state elections the proportion of voters is always considerably smaller than this. It is impossible to predict whether greater and more widespread participation would tend to reduce the intensity of our political conflicts. Probably it would not. It would, however, lead toward a fuller realization of democratic procedures in the solution of many of the political issues which divide our country today.

A third aspect of our culture in which a wide differential has given rise to divisive group loyalties is the area of education. Groupings on the basis of education bear a very close similarity to those based on economic differences, for economic level is one of the most accurate indexes of the amount of education an individual will be able to receive. The most recent figures published by the U. S. Office of Education[15] indicate that, although school attendance at all levels is increasing, there is still an enormous differential in educational attainment. The following tabulation shows the percentage of school attendance by age groups in October 1945:

Age	Percentage enrolled
5	28.3
6	93.2
7–9	98.2
10–13	97.9
14–17	78.8
18–19	20.6
20–24	3.9

[14] American Institute of Public Opinion, *The Gallup Political Almanac for 1948* (Princeton: The Institute, 1948), p. 13.

[15] U. S. Office of Education, *Biennial Survey of Education, 1944–46* (Washington: U. S. Government Printing Office, 1949), Chapter I.

In 1939–40, approximately half of the persons of high school age were graduating from high school. In 1945–46, because of the continued effects of the war, this percentage was down to 45.5. Figures for this same year show that, excluding veterans, 13 per cent of the young people of college age were enrolled in college; and only 5.7 per cent of the total population who were of graduating age were actually graduating from college.

Even with generous allowance for the effects of the war, these figures make it apparent that, measured in length of time spent in school, there is great variation in the amount of education received by individuals. Equally important is the wide range in educational facilities which may be discovered within communities and from one region to another. Figures compiled by the Institute of Administrative Research of Teachers College show that, during the year 1946–47, the various states ranged, in median expenditure per pupil, from a low of less than $30 to a high in excess of $230. In the state with the median of $230, the range extended from about $50 per pupil to about $325 per pupil.[16] While the quality of education cannot be measured alone in terms of the amount of money it costs, it seems certain that the extreme differences in educational facilities reflected by this range of expenditures are an important factor in determining the quality of education which will be possible.

Another source of variation is the great divergence in purposes and procedures which may be found in different schools and school systems. The opinions and attitudes developed by a student attending a public school in a wealthy suburb of New York City will be far different from those held by the graduate of a one-room school in rural Arkansas; and different from both of these will be the attitudes of the public school students in a poor Southern mill town. Recent developments with respect to federal aid to education have focused our attention on the differences which divide public and parochial schools. Nondenominational private schools may also be found which represent still other emphases in purposes and procedures. For example,

[16] Institute of Administrative Research, Teachers College, Columbia University, *Still Unfinished: Our Educational Obligation to America's Children* (Washington: National Education Association, 1948).

sharp contrasts will be seen in a comparison of the classical curriculum of St. John's College with the curriculum of an institution such as Bennington College, or the program of the Harvard Graduate School of Business with that of the schools maintained by the International Ladies Garment Workers Union.

It may be argued that the diversity which has been indicated here is merely a reflection of social, economic, and philosophical differences which already exist within the culture. To a great extent this is true. It is equally true, however, that these differences are brought to a sharp focus in our schools, and education is one of the primary means by which they are perpetuated. The fact that a poor child from a small town in Mississippi must go to work after six or eight years of inadequate education merely increases the improbability that he will ever achieve the same economic status as the wealthy student at Princeton or Yale, or that his political attitudes will be consistent with those of the latter. Furthermore, the education which these two individuals receive will frequently tend to spread the range of differences into other areas and thus increase the difficulty of interchange. For example, the graduate student at Yale who has specialized in comparative philology may be less able to carry on any kind of communication with a Southern sharecropper than if he had left school at the end of the sixth grade. There may be equally little common ground for exchange between a classical scholar from St. John's College and a graduate student who is specializing in agronomy. Although education has the potentiality for bridging the gaps which separate individuals and groups, it may also, and frequently does, serve to widen them.

A fourth source of divisive group loyalties which may be found within our culture is the existence of regional patterns of thought and behavior. These varying patterns originate from many factors: a difference in economies is at the basis of the historic conflict between the North and the South; a whole way of life has grown up around the cattle-raising industry of the West and the Southwest; the same may be said of the midwestern corn-belt states or the prairie states; an older and stronger tradition in the eastern states is an important factor in setting them apart from the Far West which is relatively close to its pioneer days. Another factor which gives rise to regional demarcations is the concentration of nationality or religious groups.

While it is true that regional differences may be traced to such sources, the point to be noted here is that within each region there tend to develop distinctive patterns of living which extend far beyond the original sources and which themselves elicit loyalty from the group. For example, the ideas of hospitality which predominate in Back Bay Boston, the Deep South, and a western ranch exhibit marked differences although this aspect of human relations has no more than a very tenuous connection with the basic factors of history and economy which set the regions apart. The Boston matron and the mistress of a southern plantation may be quite unaware of these more basic sources of conflict, but their variance with respect to matters of etiquette will be none the less sharp on this account. The regional pattern of living becomes a distinct thing in itself which binds the inhabitants of the region together as a group.

The increased interassociation which has come about in recent years as a result of improved methods of transportation and communication has tended both to bring these differences into sharper relief and to decrease them. Close association with a culture which is foreign to our own makes us more aware of the points at which it differs from ours. At the same time, unless the relations between the groups are completely hostile, continued association results in a give-and-take which tends to eliminate many of the sharp differentiations. While there is much evidence that the regional boundaries in this country are being thus weakened, there are still many sharp differences which are sources of conflict and division.

Differences in race and religion, constituting a fifth category, have been responsible for some of the sharpest and most bitter conflicts in our national life. The Negroes, the Jews, and the Catholics are the three groups which first come to mind when racial and religious conflicts are mentioned. But these three merely head the list, they do not exhaust it. In California the problem has centered around the Oriental and the Mexican populations; in New York City the recent influx of Puerto Ricans has been the source of some friction; in many industrial towns and mining towns, nationality groups such as the Italians and the Polish have been the objects of discrimination. Thus the list could be continued.

There is perhaps nothing that will hold a group together more tightly than the threat, or the fact, of unjust treatment from another group. As the Jews, the Catholics, the Negroes, the Mexicans, and other minority groups within the country have been excluded from full and free participation in our culture, each group has drawn more closely together, and out of the sense of exclusion and injustice has developed stronger group bonds. Thus, in the case of the Jews, for example, their sense of groupness comes not only from the fact that they share a common religion and a common tradition, but also from their feelings of exclusion, of distrust, and even of hatred for their persecutors. When animosity and suspicion provide the motivation for the maintenance of groups within a culture, the effect on the life of the culture as a whole is obviously disruptive in the extreme.

The interests of specialized vocational groups represent a sixth source of disunity and division. Vocational specialization generally carries with it a substantial group of biases and the individual tends to view all the problems of living from the point of view of his particular specialty. Let us imagine, for example, the way in which several individuals will appraise the rising divorce rate in this country. The sociologist will see it as evidence of severe social and psychological strains within the culture; to the gossip columnist it will be more grist for his mill, at least in those cases where the individuals involved have newsworthy names; for the Catholic priest it will represent a violation of God's will; the mining engineer, on the other hand, may not be particularly concerned since this phenomenon has no direct bearing on his particular vocational interests. Thus, even on a relatively impersonal level, vocational interests will give rise to widely varying points of view, and even to conflict of some intensity. Evidence may be seen of bitter disagreement between behaviorists and field theory psychologists, between psychologists and educators, between teachers and administrators, between engineers and artists, and between professional politicians and political scientists.

The disagreements indicated above arise, for the most part, out of a relatively impersonal evaluation of the facts according to the lights of a particular vocational specialty. Opposition also grows out of economic interests which bring vocational groups into conflict. Mention of this has already been made in the discussion of economic conflicts in the culture. It may be worth while here, however, to mention as further examples the long-standing struggle between educators and real estate interests with respect to taxes for the support of public schools, and the bitter fight which the American Medical Association has waged against legislation for socialized medicine. All parties concerned would certainly deny that they were motivated entirely by economic interests and this would undoubtedly be true. At the same time, it seems quite certain that economic considerations play an important part in the formation of their attitudes.

The close relationship between economic and vocational interests which has been illustrated here is only one example of the many interrelationships which exist between all the factors discussed above. Economic status, political beliefs, education, place of birth and habitation, race, religion, and vocation—all of these are intricately bound together in the life of each individual and each plays a part in determining where his loyalties lie. To the extent that groups within the culture are in conflict, the individual is set against his fellow men; to the extent that his own loyalties conflict one with another, he is set against himself.

HIGHLY COMPETITIVE CHARACTER OF THE CULTURE

Walton H. Hamilton, writing in the *Encyclopedia of the Social Sciences,* has shown how competition is an outgrowth of "the fact of rivalry [which is] universal in life and in society." [17] By a long and extremely complicated process, it has been built into our culture "as at once a process of selection, an economic organization and an agency for social development." [18] It has,

[17] Walton H. Hamilton, "Competition," *Encyclopedia of the Social Sciences* (New York: The Macmillan Company, 1937), p. 142.
[18] *Loc. cit.*

in short, become the accepted guide to successful living in our culture. According to the practical philosophy of the business world, each man must fight aggressively for what he gets. Within the rules of the game, which have been established by law and custom, the superior talent is bound to win out and thus intelligence and application are sure to receive their just reward. Because the game is open to all comers, even the best talents will be subject to constant challenge; on the one hand, this provides assurance that business will be operated at a high level of efficiency; at the same time, it prevents the development of monopolistic controls.

While the principle of competitive aggressiveness has formed the basis for the development of the American economic system, it is important to note that the great majority of individuals in our culture have but limited opportunity to engage in highly competitive practices with respect to their economic life. In this connection Lynd has said:

. . . most of us Americans are not super-aggressors, most of us are not successes-in-a-big-way, and life consists for most people in just living along. This "just-living-along" quality is a large part of American culture. But its numerical predominance does not render it either emotionally predominant or entirely emotionally self-contained. It represents, rather, in American life an enforced second-best, a coming to terms with the situation in which one finds oneself caught. At every point our young, optimistic culture thrusts forward its gains rather than its costs and losses. It plays up in print and symbol the pace-setting ways of life of its more successful members. There is a general tendency for people on all levels to struggle after these authoritative ways of living.[19]

As Lynd has pointed out, although the competitive factor plays only a very limited part in the lives of most individuals, at least with respect to their economic welfare, this is true largely through force of circumstance rather than through choice. Concentration of business and industrial enterprises has severely limited the individual's opportunities for competition in these areas. At the same time, success, in the American vocabulary, is defined to a considerable extent in terms of doing better and going further than one's neighbors, and the "self-made" man who has

[19] Lynd, *op. cit.*, pp. 73–74.

fought his way up from the bottom still looms large in the American dream. The idea of competition plays a major role in shaping our thinking and our behavior.

The existence of a competitive spirit within a culture is certainly not to be deplored. It has made enormous contributions to our growth as a nation and, with the necessary controls, will doubtless be of continuing value in our development. However, overemphasis on competition, to the exclusion of cooperative effort, is undesirable from the standpoint both of the welfare of the group and of the welfare and security of the individual. When the success of an individual or a group enterprise is thought of exclusively in terms of victory over an inimical world the result is that, despite the theoretical concept that competition contributes to the common good, in reality the idea of the common good is lost in the shuffle. Groups and individuals are caught up in a never-ending struggle in which the security of one depends upon the failure of another. The self-defeating consequences of such extreme competition are obvious and have been amply demonstrated in our economic life. The abuses of competitive enterprise have been brought under at least partial control since the tragic days of the Thirties. It seems apparent, however, that the competitive motivation is still disturbingly dominant and is one of the major sources of division and conflict within our culture.

EMPHASIS ON SPECIALIZATION

The intense specialization which is one of the outstanding characteristics of our culture has developed from two closely interrelated causes. In the first place, the field of human knowledge has increased immeasurably and at a constantly accelerating pace since the time of the Renaissance. The boundaries of our knowledge have so widened that no one person can possibly master more than a very small fraction of it. In the second place, the vast technology which has been made possible through our extended knowledge depends, to a large extent, upon the development of highly specialized skills. As the methods of technology have been taken over by other institutions, and as enterprises in all fields of endeavor have become larger and more complex, specialization has become the rule in practically all the areas of our living.

Specialization, therefore, is an inevitable fact of our existence. It has, indeed, been one of the major factors in making possible the variety, the richness, and the material comfort of contemporary living. To the extent that it has contributed to the improvement of our methods of transportation and communication it has also facilitated a wider exchange between groups and individuals. Its contribution in this respect, however, has been purely on the material level. A bond salesman living in New York City can fly to California in ten or twelve hours; in a matter of minutes he can make a telephone call or send a telegram. Thus from the material standpoint, communication with very distant points is no great problem. However, if the bond salesman engages in conversation with a fruit packer on a California ranch he may encounter some difficulty in finding a basis for very extensive interchange.

This example is given merely to illustrate the fact that as skills and knowledges have become more highly specialized, the common ground of interests and attitudes which provide the basis for mutual exchange has tended to shrink, and we find ourselves with highly efficient means, but only limited ability, for communication. As each individual pursues his highly specialized interest, such pursuit tends to become an end in itself and its possible contribution in terms of larger group values is relegated to a position of minor importance. Furthermore, complete mastery of one special field of knowledge is frequently accompanied by complete ignorance of other areas of specialization. As a result, the difficulty of maintaining contacts and associations with individuals in other fields of endeavor is greatly increased.

Reference has already been made to the conflicts which occur between groups organized in terms of vocational interests. It is unnecessary to discuss this problem further except to note that it is largely a phenomenon of specialization. In a primitive culture where a single man builds a whole house, his resistance to novel ideas will be that which men frequently exhibit toward the unfamiliar. But once he has perceived that a new technique or material will make his work easier and enable him to erect a stronger and more efficient building, he need not fear it for it will increase his comfort and security rather than threaten it. Where house-building has become highly specialized, as it has in our culture, carpenters' unions, as well as lumber interests, oppose the development of an inexpensive building brick, and all the building trades are united in their opposition to prefabricated housing, for they see in such developments a real threat to their livelihood and security.

Taking due account, therefore, of the considerable material benefits which specialization has made possible, it is necessary to recognize that it has also brought with it less fortunate results. It has been a major factor in isolating the individual from the society in which he lives and in causing disruptive frictions between groups within the culture.

LOOSENING OF GROUP BONDS DUE TO INCREASED MOBILITY

The striking developments in transportation and communication which have so greatly facilitated the material aspects of interchange within our culture have also given us a degree of mobility which is unprecedented in human history. The young man attaining maturity today is disinclined to stay at home and take over his father's farm or business; he is much more apt to go off to the city in search of bigger opportunities. Indeed, in all probability his father has no business which he can take over, and if his local community does not offer adequate employment opportunities he must, of necessity, move to a place where such opportunities are available. The great mobility of our population was most strikingly illustrated during World War II by the tremendous migrations to centers where war industries offered promise of employment.

In addition to this physical mobility the individual in our culture enjoys great freedom of movement with respect to groups and levels within the culture. This, as was pointed out earlier, is a part of the great American dream, and while the progress from rags to riches may be, in fact, harder to realize today than it once was, it is an idea that enjoys popular sanction and is influential in shaping our thinking.

This freedom of movement and association is one of the important assets of our democratic culture. It increases the flexibility of group association and provides the individual with rich opportunities for varied experiences. At the same time, however, it tends to discourage the striking of deep roots and the individual finds himself a person alone in a world of lonely people. Partly through choice and partly through force of circumstance, he does not form the strong attachments with his family, his neighbors, or his community which are characteristic of a more stable culture. The price of his "freedom" is loss of the security of group belongingness and of the experience of deep and close group association. His life has been described by Lynd in the following quotation:

The dweller in a large American city tends to be a highly developed roving predatory animal. His culture resembles a frontier boomtown, with everywhere the clatter of new buildings going up and disregard for the niceties of living in pursuit of the main chance. He is free—free to swim or to drown, free to bet all his life on "the big money," free to turn on the gas as a lost and beaten atom in the anonymity of his furnished hall-bedroom. "Man moving rapidly over the face of nature evades his destiny, which is himself. Time loses its grip on space, and space on time. . . . Plants that spread rapidly do not strike deep roots. . . ." [20]

LOSS OF FEELING OF THE INDIVIDUAL'S ROLE
AND RESPONSIBILITY IN SOCIAL LIVING

The above quotation points toward another factor in the American culture which has been disintegrative in its effects. As the individual gains greater freedom of movement and his associations become more transitory and superficial, he tends to lose any sense of responsibility for group enterprises and disassociates himself from group activities. His mobility, however, is only one of several causes for this situation. Equally important are the overwhelming size and the complexity of the organizations within our culture. In the New England town meeting, each member of the community knew that when he spoke his voice would be heard; the directness and immediacy of his participation in community affairs strengthened his sense of indi-

[20] Lynd, op. cit., pp. 79–80.

vidual importance as a responsible member of the group. By contrast, the individual living in a city of several million people is apt to despair that his small voice will carry any weight in such a vast group. Furthermore, the complexity of the machinery through which he must participate in the affairs of the community obscures the relationship between his activities and their eventual results. This aspect of our culture has been aptly described by Fromm in the following passage:

Vastness of cities in which the individual is lost, buildings that are as high as mountains, constant acoustic bombardment by the radio, big headlines changing three times a day and leaving one no choice to decide what is important, shows in which one hundred girls demonstrate their ability with clock-like precision to eliminate the individual and act like a powerful though smooth machine, the beating rhythm of jazz—these and many other details are expressions of a constellation in which the individual is confronted by uncontrollable dimensions in comparison with which he is a small particle. All he can do is to fall in step like a marching soldier or a worker on the endless belt. He can act; but the sense of independence, significance, has gone.[21]

The individual, feeling that his influence in such a vast and complex organization is negligible, loses his sense of worth and individual importance as a responsible member of the community. He therefore suffers not only the loss of meaningful association with his fellow men but also a loss of integrity and self-esteem. As for the community, it suffers a corresponding loss of vitality, and the management of its affairs falls generally into the hands of a few individuals and groups who are dominated by motives of self-interest and personal gain. Thus the ways and values of democracy are submerged.

In conclusion, it may be said that probably no situation is ever all good or all bad. While the emphasis of this discussion has been on the negative aspects of certain factors in our culture, it is true that most of these same factors have made, in varying degree, positive contributions to the life of our country. The problems of democracy cannot be solved by eliminating the differences which presently divide us, nor by an arbitrary regression to simpler and more static patterns of living. With

[21] Fromm, *op. cit.*, pp. 131-32.

respect to every aspect of our living, we must recognize both the threats and the potentialities for a better democratic society and chart our course accordingly. To do this is both the method and the purpose of general education in a democratic culture.

EMERGING CONCEPTS IN EDUCATION

The first part of this chapter has outlined the major principles of the democratic philosophy which serve as guide lines for American education. While these principles provide a broad context within which our educational institutions must operate, it is still necessary to determine how schools can best serve the aims of a democratic society and what their relation to the social order will be. These considerations, by and large, constitute the subject matter of educational philosophy. The implementation of a philosophy of education, furthermore, depends to a considerable degree upon the theories of learning which accompany it. Without attempting a complete survey of either of these fields, the present discussion will indicate briefly some of the major concepts in educational philosophy and in the psychology of learning which have had a marked influence on the development of the general education movement.

EDUCATION BASIC TO THE DEMOCRATIC WAY OF LIFE

In any social order, education has a role of major significance. This statement implies a definition of education which includes all the experiences an individual may have which will help to shape his subsequent behavior—even the absence or withholding of experiences. An autocratic society which depends for its survival on the suppression of intelligence must exercise extreme care in controlling the experiences of its members and must insure, above all, that such experiences as would tend toward the liberation of the intelligence will be withheld. While it is true that, in the light of the democratic philosophy, this will be considered as mis-education rather than education, still, in terms of an autocratic philosophy, it may be the best possible kind of education. Therefore, merely to say that education is basic to the democratic way of life has little meaning unless we understand the democratic conception of the individual and his relation to society, for it is from this concept that all ideas of education are derived.

Because these are the focal points around which any concept of education revolves, it may be worth while to refer back to the earlier discussion of the democratic philosophy long enough to reiterate several points that were made there:

1. Every individual is to be regarded always as an end and never as a means.
2. In this respect all men are to stand equal.
3. The ultimate purpose of the democratic society is the liberation of the individual's potentialities for creative, intelligent, self-disciplined living.
4. There is an interdependent relationship between individual living and group living whereby each contributes to the richness and the vitality of the other and, conversely, neither can prosper without the other.
5. The individual and the group likewise bear a mutual responsibility each for the welfare of the other.

These statements indicate, in a general way, the functions which education assumes in a democratic society. While all the institutions in a democracy are to be conceived in terms of the welfare of its citizens, it is the particular function of education to foster the maximum growth of every individual to the end that he will be capable of intelligent, creative, self-disciplined behavior. The idea of creativity and self-discipline as desirable, and even necessary, ends is one of the most distinctive characteristics of a democratic philosophy of education, for democracy may be distinguished from authoritarian theories of social organization mainly by the fact that it must depend upon the voluntary contributions of all its citizens for its maintenance and improvement.

This being the case, it follows logically that a democratic society must provide all its citizens with equal educational opportunities. The idea of equality, as it is used here, does not mean that all individuals should have the same kind of education but, rather, that education, together with the other agencies of society, must be devoted to the full realization of each individual's potentialities. This concept necessitates a high degree of individualization of education both in kind and in amount. While it is true, as someone has said, that human beings are more alike than they are different, still, the democratic philosophy recognizes each individual as a unique personality, and to this extent his educational experiences should be unique.

It should be noted here that the idea of individualization of education does not receive universal support from contemporary authorities in education. Dissent has arisen in particular from the Classicists and the neo-Thomists whose attitudes on this point have been expressed by Hutchins in this frequently quoted passage:

Education implies teaching. Teaching implies knowledge. Knowledge is truth. The truth is everywhere the same. Hence, education should be everywhere the same.[22]

In reference to a similar statement by Mark Van Doren, Hook has effectively pointed out the fallacy of this educational concept in the following statement:

What this [Van Doren's statement that liberal education should be the same for all people] says is that if we know what the end of education should be, then the means in every case must be the same no matter how different the individuals whom we are to educate. This is like saying that, since the aim of medicine is to produce health for everybody, if the best diet is known there is no individual whom it will not fit, and each should have all of it. In medicine, an argument of this kind is an unfailing mark of a quack. From the truth that medicine has a common end for everybody it does not follow that there is a common means of achieving it independently of whether a person has diabetes or leukemia, is thin or fat.[23]

Equality of education, according to the point of view expressed by Hook, does not mean providing the same educational experiences for every individual regardless of his particular characteristics; quite the contrary, it means providing an education which is conceived in terms of these characteristics. The com-

[22] Robert M. Hutchins, *The Higher Learning in America* (New Haven: Yale University Press, 1936), p. 66.
[23] Sidney Hook, *Education for Modern Man* (New York: Dial Press, 1946), p. 205.

mon aim is the maximum growth of the individual for rich and meaningful living. The means must be varied according to the individual.

If the five democratic principles summarized above imply an education directed toward meaningful individual living, they carry an equally strong implication that education must be concerned with intelligent and constructive group living. In the prior discussion of democratic philosophy the relationship which the individual bears to the group and the nature of his responsibility for the welfare of the group have been sufficiently explored so that further comment here is unnecessary except to point out the central position which education assumes in the development of these individual-group relationships. One further aspect of the problem which has not yet been discussed is of sufficient importance to deserve separate treatment. This has to do with the nature of the relationship between the school and the social order.

EDUCATION FOR SOCIAL STABILITY VS. EDUCATION FOR SOCIAL CHANGE

Bertrand Russell, in *Education and the Modern World*, has drawn a sharp distinction between the education of the good individual and the education of the good citizen.

The cultivation of the individual mind is not, on the face of it, the same thing as the production of the useful citizen. Goethe, for example, was a less useful citizen than James Watt, but as an individual must be reckoned superior. There is such a thing as the good of the individual as distinct from a little fraction of the good of the community. . . .
. . . the individual as such is self-subsistent, while the citizen is essentially circumscribed by his neighbors. . . . The fundamental characteristic of the citizen is that he cooperates, in intention if not in fact. . . . Citizens as conceived by governments are persons who admire the *status quo* and are prepared to exert themselves for its preservation.[24]

While Russell subsequently acknowledges that the idea of citizenship embodied in these statements is a destructively nar-

[24] Bertrand Russell, *Education and the Modern World* (New York: W. W. Norton and Co., 1932), pp. 10–13.

row one, there is the strong implication here that the educational ideal of the state is directed exclusively toward the maintenance of the *status quo*. It is certainly true that, as Brubacher has pointed out, this is a time-honored theory of the function of education.

By far the oldest theory of the mutual relations of the school and the social order, and the one most widely honored in practice, is that the school should conserve the existing social culture . . . except culture patterns be conserved through the school, there is no way to shorten the period of trial and error which is incident and precedent to social progress. Especially is it important for the school to perform this conservative function if other social institutions neglect to do so.[25]

Brubacher continues his discussion by pointing out that the conservative function of education is not necessarily to be identified with reactionary forms of social organization alone, that "it is entirely possible for the school to conserve social systems of the left as well as those of the right, radical ones as well as reactionary ones."[26]

Kallen has pushed the argument one step further by demonstrating that the school inevitably serves, to some extent, a conservative function.

Without memory, no personality and no biography; and by the same token, no social unity, no national character and national ideal, no history. And if no history, no insight into the dynamic of the process of the national life, then no adequacy in controlling the present and shaping the future. In a very obvious sense there is no education which is not historical education. For no matter how passionately, how aggressively, education may be directed toward the future, it is so directed only as it makes the past available, and successfully directed only as it makes available the truth of the past.[27]

The idea of change carries with it the idea of a present condition, the present condition here being the accumulation of the culture. Except as this accumulation of the culture is a part of

[25] By permission from *Modern Philosophies of Education*, p. 187, by John S. Brubacher. Copyright, 1939. McGraw-Hill Book Company, Inc.

[26] *Ibid.*, p. 188.

[27] *The Education of Free Men*, p. 104. Copyright, 1949, by Horace M. Kallen; Farrar, Straus and Young, Inc., publishers.

education there can be no possibility of change. Education without reference to a past, or with a completely negative reference to the past, is unthinkable. The question, therefore, is not whether the school should or should not have a conservative function, since this, to some degree at least, is inescapable. It is rather whether, from society's viewpoint, this should be its sole function. And if this question is answered negatively, then we may ask to what extent the state can countenance education which is critical of its institutions and which is directed toward change.

Brubacher has pointed out that strong arguments have been presented that the school cannot be a powerful agent of social change, that this is the function of much more elemental forces such as invention, war, economic conflict, and racial migration. According to this theory the function of the school is to consolidate the changes which have been instituted by these other forces if and when they have received the sanction of society. "In this view, the school is the servant of social change, not its master." [28]

However, the question of whether or not the school can be instrumental in effecting social change seems to revolve primarily around the question of whether it can hope to receive the support of a community except as it is wholeheartedly devoted to the perpetuation of that community. This is not a question which can be settled with any finality in the abstract because it is contingent upon a number of variables in the particular situation having to do primarily with the kind of relationship which exists between the school and the community, and the extent to which the community accepts the democratic idea of a constantly evolving social order. In this respect it is important to note that the community owes an obligation to the school, for as Brubacher has said, "The school is one of the community's resources for social experimentation and, as such, should not be neglected. What the supporters of [the] critical theory [of education] seek is not an alienation of the school from life, but protection in a freedom to study life independently. If freedom were the settled policy of the schools no matter what factor

[28] Brubacher, *op. cit.*, pp. 194-95.

commanded a political majority, the educational policy of the schools would not suffer convulsions when political power would periodically change hands." [29]

In terms of the democratic philosophy, the solution to this problem seems to involve two things: first, that the school should be free "to study life independently"—to view openly and with the least possible bias all aspects of the culture; and second, that it should foster in its students the development of a critical intelligence which will be capable of constructive evaluation and responsible action. The role of the democratic school in social reconstruction has been admirably stated by the authors of *The Educational Frontier:*

We are concerned . . . that the process of education from beginning to end operate so that students think their own thoughts and live their own lives, but with an ever growing appreciation of the significance of their conduct as bearing upon the lives of others. Our view starts with a respect for the integrity of the individual, and it ends by placing upon the next generation the responsibility and the opportunity for arriving at more adequate solutions of life's problems than now we see. To the extent that the school is successful in bringing about a reorganization of its life in this direction it will contribute directly toward a more tolerant and humane social order, toward a way of life that approaches the democratic ideal.[30]

EDUCATION AS A DEMOCRATIC PROCESS

While it has long been acknowledged that education is essential to successful democratic living, only recently has it been recognized that education itself should be a democratic process. This point of view may be said to represent the growing edge of educational thought for in the great majority of our schools we are still faced with the contradiction of authoritarian education devoted to the preservation of a democratic way of life. The aim of a democratic society is democratic control of all its agencies and institutions; thus the existence of an autocratic education within our society constitutes a denial of the principles

[29] *Ibid.*, p. 191.
[30] William H. Kilpatrick and others, *The Educational Frontier* (New York: D. Appleton-Century Company, 1933), pp. 211–12.

we subscribe to. In addition to this obvious contradiction, there are at least three further arguments for the democratic control of education; the first stems from the principle of a democratic philosophy; the other two have to do with the nature of human learning.

We have seen that an inherent characteristic of the philosophy which has been described here is the belief in the right and the ability of the individual to manage his own affairs—to set his goals and to determine the means of attaining them. In fact, it is one of the chief responsibilities of democratic education to foster the development of independent, self-disciplined behavior. A close corollary of this belief in the right of the individual for self-determination is the concept that all individuals who participate in, or are affected by, the activities of an institution should have an active part in its control and management. The implication which these beliefs carry for education seems clear. In the first place, the control of the school is broadened to include all members of the community. To the extent that parents, taxpayers, administrators, teachers, and students are involved with the activities of education, they should have the right and the obligation to participate in the control of its affairs. With particular reference to curriculum planning, Krug has written:

Involved in educational planning at any time are the following groups: (1) state-wide leadership groups; (2) local leadership groups; (3) classroom teachers; (4) lay people; (5) children and youth in school. Not one of these groups is equipped to do the whole job of curriculum development. Likewise, not one of these groups can or should be left out. But it is equally true that these groups are not equally fitted to participate in all . . . of the major curriculum development tasks. A major problem of curriculum development practice today is so to organize the program that each group will take part in that phase where it can make an effective contribution.[31]

What Krug has said here with respect to curriculum development may be applied to all aspects of educational planning. Each group in the community has certain unique contributions

[31] Edward A. Krug, *Curriculum Planning* (New York: Harper and Brothers, 1950), pp. 8–9.

which it can make to the development of the educational program. To ignore these contributions can result only in eventual loss both to the school and to society.

The role of community groups, at least with respect to certain policies and procedures of education, has long been recognized. It is only recently, however, that serious attention has been given to the part which students should have in educational planning. This is a highly controversial field in which there are many shades of opinion. At one extreme we have the strict authoritarians whose point of view has been expressed by Adler when he writes that "the aim of education should be the same for all men . . . the ends of education are absolute and universal." [32] While the proponents of this point of view do not necessarily claim to have discovered completely either the universal aims or the means for achieving them, they do believe that through logical processes such aims and means can be discovered. The role of the student is one of complete acceptance. While he may be free to question, it is argued that he will, if he is capable of clear, logical thought, arrive at precisely the same conclusions as his teachers.

In opposition to this point of view is the position which has been most commonly identified with the philosophy of experimentalism which holds that all truths are relative and that therefore universal aims or means do not, and cannot, exist. Furthermore, the experimentalist theory of education as experience places great emphasis on the need for the individual to select his own goals and direct his own learning experiences. Those who support this point of view do so, first, on the basis of the argument that this is the democratic right of every individual. The function of the school is not to control and dictate the learning of students but rather to foster a continuous growth in the ability to set worthy goals and work with intelligence toward their achievement.

The second argument for the democratic control of education stems from the theory that learning takes place only as

[32] Mortimer J. Adler, "In Defense of the Philosophy of Education," *Philosophies of Education*, Forty-first Yearbook of the National Society for the Study of Education, Part I (Chicago: The Society, 1942), p. 244.

learning activities are directed toward a goal which the learner himself understands and regards as important. This viewpoint has been summarized by Kilpatrick as follows:

Each one learns his responses, only his responses; he learns all his responses as he accepts them to act on, some to do, others to ignore; he learns his responses in the degree that they are important to him and in the further degree that they are interrelated with what he already knows.[33]

This makes it not only desirable but necessary that the learner should share in the planning of his learning activities, for, as Kilpatrick says,

. . . if the child or the adult learner is to learn an idea, that idea must (before it can be learned) spring up in the child's mind as his response, his thinking response, to a situation which he confronts. I, as a teacher, may help that particular idea to arise in his mind, but he learns it as an idea only as it constitutes his response to the situation which calls it forth. I can help him, but I cannot simply hand him an idea and tell him to learn it.[34]

It is sometimes objected that this position favors a condition of chaos, or at least leads to such a condition, in which each individual pursues selfishly conceived goals without respect for the welfare of the group. While it is true that an overemphasis on individual goals has sometimes led to such unfortunate results, the kind of education envisaged here, when properly conceived, goes on in a context of group relationships and one of its most important aims is to help the learner grow in the understanding of his role as a member of the group.

With a slightly different emphasis, this same concept may be applied to the role of the teacher in the learning situation. He too must understand and accept as his own the goals toward which a learning situation is directed and the methods which are employed to achieve them. Teaching by prescription is as certain of failure as learning by prescription.

The third argument for education as a democratic process is

[33] William H. Kilpatrick, "Philosophy of Education from the Experimentalist Outlook," *Philosophies of Education*, Forty-first Yearbook of the National Society for the Study of Education, Part I (Chicago: The Society, 1942, pp. 68–69.
[34] *Loc. cit.*

related to the idea that learning is most effective when it results from actual doing. We may turn again to Kilpatrick for an expression of this principle:

. . . our young people can learn democracy only as they live democracy. It cannot be taught by indoctrination for that is an essentially undemocratic process. Our schoolrooms must then become living democracies as far as is feasible with children and youth. It may further be added that the schoolrooms can hardly be living democracies unless the school systems are themselves living democracies.[35]

EDUCATION INVOLVES THE TOTAL ORGANISM

Traditionally, the purpose of education has been conceived primarily as the cultivation of the mind through the transmission of knowledges and skills. In recent years, a variety of factors have operated to reveal the inadequacy of this concept of education. Psychological research has shown that, as Murray states, "thinking is a function of the entire personality, rather than an isolated faculty," [36] so that even in the realm of purely intellectual learning, the total organism is involved. At the same time, earlier theories regarding the learning process—the theory of transfer of training on the one hand and the psychology of connectionism on the other—are giving way to an organismic view which regards learning as essentially the development of relationships. According to this view, learning is meaningful only as the learner is able to relate it to the larger configuration of his total pattern of living.

Along with these changes in our theories about how learning takes place, there have been profound cultural changes which have altered the functions and the responsibilities of education. In a simpler culture, many aspects of an individual's education are adequately cared for in his out-of-school life by such institutions as the home, the community, and the church. In our highly complex and, in many respects, less integrated culture, these institutions have been unable to provide adequate educational experiences and the responsibilities of the school have been

[35] *Ibid.*, p. 78.
[36] H. A. Murray, *Explorations in Personality* (New York: Oxford University Press, 1938), p. 740.

thus broadened and increased. At the same time, the rapidly increasing enrollment in our schools has brought about a change in the nature of the school population. This change, in recent years, has perhaps been most marked at the secondary and college levels. Whereas these levels of education were at one time available only to the economically privileged, the opportunities for high school and college education are gradually being extended to those who are less favored in this respect. A liberal education for the cultural elite is one thing; a functional education for democratic living is quite another, for it shifts the emphasis from the cultivation of intellectual virtues as an end in itself to the entire range of personal-social needs which confront the individual in a democratic culture.

For these reasons there is a growing tendency to look far beyond the mere transmission of knowledges and skills as the total function of education to an idea of education as involved with the growth and development of the total personality. It is concerned therefore with emotion as well as intellect, physical health as well as mental health, esthetic interests as well as scientific interests, and with all the needs of the individual as a member of a family, a worker, and a member of the social group. In short, education is concerned with all those factors which contribute to the healthy growth and development of the total personality.

Chapter III

THE PURPOSES OF GENERAL EDUCATION

The discussion to this point has endeavored, first, to provide a definition of general education and, second, to explore those factors in the American culture which have been most instrumental in determining the course of its development. It now remains to indicate more specifically what the purposes of general education are. As has been indicated, its ultimate objective is to help each individual achieve a rich and satisfying personal life in which he will make the maximum contribution to the life of the group. But a statement as broad and abstract as this can mean all things to all people. As Bigelow and MacLean have pointed out, "College catalogs dating back over many decades reveal numberless statements of broad objectives with which general education today could hardly quarrel." "But," they continue, "there are two difficulties with these statements. First they are couched in high order abstractions, which the reader can hardly interpret exactly. Second, modern educators suspect that there was often in the past insufficient demonstrable relation between these objectives and the procedures employed for their presumable attainment." [1] It is therefore necessary to state in more specific terms the kind of behavior which general education seeks to promote.

The final test of any education is the kind of behavior which results from it. A course in typing, for example, may be based on the loftiest educational and philosophical principles, but unless the students who take it come away with the ability to type with a reasonable amount of speed and accuracy, it must be judged a poor course. Likewise, the test of general education is the extent to which it is productive of worthy individual and group living. Since it is the behavior of individuals with which we are ultimately concerned, it is in terms of behavior that the purposes of general education can be most directly stated. On the other hand, it must be recognized that a behavioral description of educational purposes, if stated in too specific terms, can be even more harmful than one which remains at the level of vague generalities. Purposes may be stated more specifically for a particular group of thirty students than for a total college student body, just as they can be stated more specifically for a particular student body than for all the college students in the nation. The following discussion, therefore, attempts to indicate, with respect to the major areas of activity which are the concern of general education, the kind of behavior which is consistent with a democratic philosophy of living.

1. *It is the purpose of general education to develop in the individual a critical loyalty to democratic ideals and to foster behavior consistent with a belief in these ideals.*

This aim involves, first of all, the individual's personal relationships with his fellow men—with his family, his friends, his working associates. Happy and successful personal living depends upon the development of a code of ethics in the contacts which the individual makes in the course of his daily living; such ethical personal relationships, furthermore, are at the basis of successful group life. As the President's Commission has stated,

[1] Karl W. Bigelow and Malcolm S. MacLean, "Dominant Trends in General Education," *General Education in the American College*, Thirty-eighth Yearbook of the National Society for the Study of Education, Part II (Bloomington: Public School Publishing Co., 1939), p. 362.

"Interpersonal relations, business relations, labor relations, even international relations, depend, if they are to prosper, on good faith, decent intentions, and mutual confidence. . . . To cooperate for common ends, we must have faith in each other." [2] Basic to the democratic concept of ethical behavior are personal integrity and honesty, a genuine respect for the human personality, tolerance for attitudes and beliefs which are at variance with one's own, a disposition to trust the other person's motives, and the desire and will to live and to work cooperatively.

It has been one of the most glaring shortcomings of our educational system that it has concerned itself almost entirely with the search for knowledge and has done too little to develop the beliefs and attitudes which will give such knowledge its true significance. All too often, in fact, it has confused objectivity and the unbiased pursuit of knowledge with inactivity and withdrawal. If the purpose of the college is to develop worthy citizens of a democratic society, then it must above all endeavor to foster a critical loyalty to the ideals of democracy, and a sense of responsibility on the part of the individual for active participation in social and political affairs.

2. *It is the purpose of general education to develop an active interest in, and an expanding knowledge about, the individual's environment—physical, social, and cultural.*

Intelligent action in any situation is contingent upon an understanding of the situation. Because successful democratic living is so largely dependent upon intelligent action, it is of primary importance that the individual should know about and understand the world in which he lives. General education must help the student, first, to understand that intelligent action is informed action, and, then, to acquire the knowledge and understanding necessary for intelligent conduct of his personal life and for worthy participation in social and political affairs.

The accelerating extension of the limits of human knowledge makes this objective continually more difficult to attain, and it is obviously impossible for the individual to acquire an extensive

---

[2] The President's Commission on Higher Education, *Higher Education in American Democracy* (New York: Harper and Brothers, 1948), I, p. 49.

knowledge of all the aspects of his environment. However, the increasing complexities of living put continually greater demands on the individual, and if he is to have a life of varied contacts and associations it is essential that he have a general knowledge of the physical, social, and cultural world in which he lives.

In addition to the objective necessity for such knowledge in the individual's daily activities, there is another perhaps less tangible value which has to do with the development of the individual's sense of selfhood. The person without an environment is a world in himself and he has no outside criteria against which he can measure himself. As his world expands, he not only sees its component parts in new relationships, he also sees himself in new relationships and thus gets new insights into his own personality.

It should be emphasized that it is less important for the college to give the student particular items of knowledge than it is to develop in him a sense of curiosity and interest in the world in which he lives. This spirit of inquiry will lead him to continued exploration and to an ever-increasing understanding of the world and of himself.

3. *It is the purpose of general education to foster the growth of a healthy social and emotional life.*

Reference has already been made to the increasing emphasis in general education upon the development of the whole personality. The well-educated person, in addition to his intellectual achievements, is characterized by social and emotional maturity. The strains and conflicts of emotional instability are extremely detrimental to effective learning, so that even if the college were solely concerned with the development of intellectual powers, it would be important to give attention to these conditioning factors. Social and emotional adjustment assume even greater importance, however, when the college frames its purposes, not merely in terms of intellectual achievement, but in terms of happy and effective living. Unless the individual has an internal sense of security and stability, and unless he is able to achieve mutually satisfactory relations with other people, his own potentialities are wasted and his contribution to the group life is, at best, a partial one and, at the worst, a negative one.

It is extremely important, therefore, that the student should gain an understanding of human behavior, with respect to both himself and his relations with other people. He should be able to pursue his college life in an atmosphere of security—security in his relationships with other people and in his achievements as a student. He should have the benefit of counseling and guidance when he needs help in solving his problems, whether they relate to his personal life, his educational adjustment, or his vocational plans. Perhaps most important of all, the college community should offer opportunity for rich and varied contacts which will help to build the student's own sense of security and integrity and will give him valuable experience in constructive personal relationships.

4. *It is the purpose of general education to foster intelligent behavior with respect to the problems of physical health.*

What has been said regarding the importance of a healthy emotional adjustment as it affects the student's total development applies with equal force to his physical well-being. The effects of poor health on intellectual achievement have been amply demonstrated at all age levels, but our colleges in particular have been slow to realize the significance of this relationship in terms of their instructional programs. In addition to recognizing the importance of physical health as it affects intellectual achievement, it is essential that it be understood as an end significant in its own right for the total development of the individual. Physical well-being, moreover, far from being a purely personal problem, is a matter of vital social concern for, as the President's Commission has stated, "In any society human resources are of paramount importance, and when the physical health and vitality of any large proportion of the people are less than they might be, these resources are seriously impaired." [3]

It is important, therefore, that the student should, first of all, develop an understanding of the importance of physical health and well-being for satisfactory personal and social living. The

[3] President's Commission, *op. cit.*, p. 54.

college must furthermore foster the development of attitudes and habits, based on reliable information, which are essential for the maintenance and improvement of the health of the individual and the community.

5. *It is the purpose of general education to develop the capacity for, and the habit of, critical and constructive thinking.*

Intelligent action, which is the basis of satisfactory living in a democratic society, can be achieved only as the result of critical, constructive thinking. Therefore, as the President's Commission has put it, "Development of the reasoning faculty, of the habit of critical appraisal, should be the constant and pervasive aim of all education, in every field and at every level." [4] Much of traditional education has been so preoccupied with imparting specific items of information that the student has had little or no opportunity to develop the skills of inquiry and critical evaluation. As a result he has been poorly equipped to meet life situations for which he has had to devise his own solutions.

More important than any specific information which the college may transmit to its students is the ability, and the predisposition, to meet situations with intelligent, critical, and constructive behavior. This involves, first of all, the development of a spirit of curiosity and inquiry, an eagerness to understand the factors relevant to any situation. It means, in the second place, the ability to analyze situations, to see what the relevant factors are and how they are related. In the third place, it necessitates the ability to evaluate the situation in terms of acceptable criteria. And lastly, it involves the ability to plan a course of action in terms of the observed facts as they have been evaluated.

While such courses as logic and mathematics may be most helpful in learning the *processes* of critical thinking, students will learn *habits* of critical thinking only as they have the opportunity to do so in all their college pursuits. In all college activities, students should be challenged to discover, to analyze, to evaluate, and to act independently. The educated man is not the man who has a set of ready-made solutions; he is the man who

[4] *Ibid.*, p. 57.

knows how to go about finding solutions to the problems which he meets.

6. *It is the purpose of general education to foster a creative approach to the problems of living.*

In our highly mechanized and standardized society, the average individual's opportunities for creative thought and action have been seriously curtailed. The material goods of his living are mass-produced for his selection; and lest he have any doubt about which radio to buy or which kind of a suit to wear, there are publications by research specialists that will tell him which one is most pleasingly designed and which gives the most efficient service. Decorators and home magazines tell him how to furnish his house and theater critics tell him what to think about the play he saw last week. The news is analyzed for him by commentators, and book clubs select his reading. The awe with which he regards the expert and the specialist, combined with his natural timidity to be different from his neighbors, operates to shape his thinking and behaving into patterns which are very near to stereotypes. This is not to say that the individual should not give due regard to the information which is available to him from experts, or that there is any particular virtue in merely being different (although even this may at times be of some value). The individual certainly cannot hope to arrive at intelligent solutions to his problems if he disregards the information of the specialist; but, having weighed the information, he must use his own ingenuity and creative originality to find the solution which is right for him as a unique individual.

Complete dependence on the word of the specialist and on the approval of the group has two highly unfortunate results. First, it reduces the individual to a state of utter dependence upon the advice and sanction of others. He may be highly intelligent in the manner in which he goes about securing information and advice, but his solutions will be borrowed solutions and his creative powers will go unchallenged. In the second place, such dependence results in a deadening uniformity and robs life of its vitality and interest. As Kallen has said, "The creative imagination brings up alternatives of idea and form; it makes new deliverances, passionate and beautiful." [5] The development of creative powers, therefore, results inevitably in enrichment and variety in living.

While the college should encourage intelligent action based on the best available evidence, it must also encourage creative action based on the individual's unique sense of relationships. This necessitates, first of all, a confidence, on the part of the student, in his own ways of thinking and working. While his mind must remain open to new evidence, he must have confidence in his ability to evaluate it and to seek new solutions to the problems which he faces. In the second place, it demands an eagerness to experiment and to try out, to seek new ways of thinking and doing which will lead to new and better patterns of living. By encouraging an attitude of creativity and inventiveness, the college will make a real contribution to the realization of the individual's potentialities for growth and to the variety and richness of the group life.

7. *It is the purpose of general education to foster active participation in the arts and esthetic sensitivity to all aspects of the environment.*

The college traditionally has given but slight attention to the role of the arts in human living so far as its actual program is concerned. While it has almost universally acknowledged that the arts represent some of the greatest achievements of man, there is little evidence that this belief has had any influence in shaping its curriculum. It has been chiefly preoccupied with the development of intellectual powers and the pursuit of scientific truth. As McGrath has pointed out, "A cultivation of the theoretical, in the special sense of a scientific search for truth, is often declared the principal function of the university." [6] This is, at one and the same time, a reflection of one of the dominant trends of our culture and a powerful force for its perpetuation. An almost total neglect of the esthetic-emotional aspects of experience is one of the most striking features of the modern scientifically oriented world.

[5] Horace M. Kallen, *Art and Freedom* (New York: Duell, Sloan, and Pearce, 1942), II, p. 907. Copyright, 1942, by Horace M. Kallen.
[6] McGrath and others, *op. cit.*, p. 180.

The second part of this volume will be devoted to an investigation of the role of the arts in human living. Therefore, it may suffice here to say that if the role of general education is conceived to be the development of the individual's total personality, then far greater attention must be given to his esthetic-emotional life. It is essential, first of all, that he be given access to those avenues of emotional expression and growth which are opened through participation in the arts. To the extent that each person has a life of feeling and emotion which has significance in its own right, he has the capacity and the urge for creative expression in the arts. This need must be met if the college is to produce healthy, well-rounded personalities.

The development of esthetic sensitivity adds new dimensions to the individual's perception of the world in which he lives. It gives him new insights into the cultural heritage from which he springs; it shows him new facets of the physical world in which he lives; it increases his understanding of other people and thereby gives him a broader basis for communication; and it gives him the ability and the will to build a more satisfying environment and a more harmonious world. The development and the maintenance of a rich artistic life within our culture depends upon the interest and the effort of all our people; to the extent that they contribute to it they will receive and appreciate its rewards. It is one of the most crucial tasks of general education to give due attention to esthetic-emotional needs and thus restore to our civilization a more balanced way of living.

8. *It is the purpose of general education to provide the knowledges and skills which the individual needs to live a wholesome and constructive family life.*

Despite the important role that marriage and family life play in our culture, education at all levels has had but little direct concern with this area of living except as it has been studied by specialists in such fields as psychology and sociology. It is as though we had assumed that the individual, in the normal course of his living, would acquire the knowledges and skills which he needs to live happily as the member of a family. However, as the President's Commission has stated, "That success in marriage and child rearing does not follow automatically from competence in other spheres is abundantly evident from the broken marriages, broken homes, and maladjusted children that are becoming all too common in America." [7] It is gradually being recognized that successful family membership is dependent upon a number of knowledges, skills, and attitudes which the individual frequently does not acquire unless efforts are directed specifically toward that end.

Because the family is one of the basic units of our cultural life, it is of the utmost importance that the present tide toward its disintegration should be stemmed. It is undoubtedly true that many of the factors which have tended to weaken it are too deeply imbedded in the culture to be entirely overcome by such educational experiences as lie within the scope of the college. But this by no means weakens the argument for including such experiences in the general education program. In the first place, despite these deeper causes for the weakening of family ties, the fact still remains that successful family membership necessitates certain individual learnings which cannot be left to chance. Furthermore, a direct study of family relationships, by focusing attention on these larger cultural problems, will create that awareness which is the first requisite for correcting them.

9. *It is the purpose of general education to provide the orientation necessary for a wise choice of vocation.*

The definition of general education which was offered in Chapter I established the distinction between general education and that part of a student's education which is concerned specifically with his competence in a vocation. It was pointed out, furthermore, that the distinction between general education and special education is not a clear-cut one; in at least two respects general education is concerned with the student's vocational plans, for it must provide him with the necessary orientation for making a wise vocational choice.

First, the individual must be capable of an honest and accurate evaluation of his own potentialities as a basis for choosing a vocation. Super has indicated the great disparity which frequently

[7] President's Commission, *op. cit.,* p. 56.

exists between a student's vocational choices and the realities of his own capacities and of the vocational field by showing that the preponderance of choices is in the middle and upper categories of the occupational scale.[8] Students tend to select those areas which have the most prestige, require the most education, and offer the highest financial returns, without due regard to the capacities and the training which success in such areas entails. Choice of a field in which a student has little chance of success leads inevitably to frustration and bitter disappointment. It also happens frequently that a student, for such reasons as parental pressure or great admiration for a particular person, will select a vocational field for which he may have the intellectual ability but for which he is unsuited temperamentally. This carries equally serious threats to his future happiness. It is exceedingly important, therefore, that the college should help him to gain a true picture of himself so that he may choose a vocational field which is in line with his particular aptitudes and abilities.

The second major task of general education in this area is to give the student an orientation with respect to the possibilities of vocational choice. He should have some idea of the range of vocations, their requirements in terms of special aptitudes and training, the income which can be expected from them, and the relative demand for personnel. In the words of the President's Commission, "The student should be helped to choose his vocation on a more objective and sensible basis than the ambitions of his parents, his own wishful thinking, or incomplete occupational information." [9] General education can make a great contribution toward the realization of this goal.

[8] Donald E. Super, *The Dynamics of Vocational Adjustment* (New York: Harper and Brothers, 1942), pp. 12 ff.
[9] President's Commission, *op. cit.*, p. 57.

Part Two

ART,
THE INDIVIDUAL,
AND SOCIETY

Chapter IV

ART IN THE LIFE OF THE INDIVIDUAL

The evidence is all too abundant that in our culture esthetic experience is generally regarded as being outside the realm of our daily pursuits, that it is the questionable privilege of a small number of individuals who are marked by their deviation from the norm. As McGrath has pointed out, "The aesthetic is not a factor in what people call common sense. It is the offspring of a very uncommon sense in the minds of most Americans. . . ." [1] And yet, as Kallen has shown, esthetic experience is a much more common phenomenon than is generally recognized even by those who have made it their special way of life:

The estheticians hardly realize how common is the experience, how frequent. Plain people are as surprised and pleased about it as was Molière's M. Jourdain when he learned that all his life he had been talking prose. It comes to them nameless, undefined by verbal markers and unaltered by esthetician's palaver, so that they live it through without classifying it, just as they breathe.[2]

[1] Earl J. McGrath and others, *Toward General Education* (New York: The Macmillan Company, 1948), p. 181.
[2] Horace M. Kallen, *Art and Freedom* (New York: Duell, Sloan, and Pearce, 1942), II, p. 949. Copyright, 1942, by Horace M. Kallen.

This statement seems to imply a point of view that, whether or not we recognize esthetic experience as such, it is, in fact, a part of the fabric of our daily lives. At the same time, it is clear that not all experience is esthetic; and many of the events in our lives, even though they have an esthetic quality, are of a predominantly practical nature. What, then, are the characteristics which distinguish esthetic experience from ordinary experience? What is the source of the esthetic factor in our living? And what relationship does esthetic experience bear to art experience? If they are not the same, wherein does their difference lie? The present chapter will attempt to find answers to these questions.

ART AND HUMAN EXPERIENCE

THE ESTHETIC QUALITY IN EXPERIENCE

All of life is experience; it may be varied or monotonous, scattered and diffused or intense, pleasurable or repugnant; but whatever the characteristics of the specific experiences in a lifetime may be, it is certain that, from the first breath to the last, all of living is experiencing. The experiences which we undergo take on meaning as they occur or are consciously organized into patterns in which the component parts of a situation have a meaningful relationship to each other and to what has gone before. Thus, Dewey, in *Art as Experience*, distinguishes between having experience and having *an* experience. The difference is summarized in the following quotation:

Oftentimes . . . the experience had is inchoate. Things are experienced, but not in such a way that they are composed into *an* experience. There is distraction and dispersion; what we observe and what we think, what we desire and what we get, are at odds with each other. We put our hands to the plow and turn back; we start and then we stop, not because the experience has reached the end for the sake of which it was initiated but because of extraneous interruptions or of inner lethargy.

In contrast with such experience, we have *an* experience when the material experienced runs its course to fulfillment. Then and then only is it integrated within and demarcated in the general stream of experience from other experiences. A piece of work is finished in a way that is satisfactory; a problem receives its solution;

a game is played through; a situation, whether that of eating a meal, playing a game of chess, carrying on a conversation, writing a book, or taking part in a political campaign, is so rounded out that its close is a consummation and not a cessation. Such an experience is a whole and carries with it its own individualizing quality and self-sufficiency. It is *an* experience.[3]

An experience in this sense is perceived as a unity in which all the parts are interrelated and all contribute to the realization of the whole. It is this quality of organization, of interrelatedness of parts in the formation of a unified totality, that gives experience its esthetic quality. Herbert Read has expressed this idea in saying that "life itself, in its most secret and essential sources, is aesthetic—that it only *is* in virtue of the embodiment of energy in a form which is not only material, but aesthetic." [4] In other words, life is possible only to the extent that it has organization and pattern, that its varied parts are functionally and dynamically interrelated—in short, to the extent that it has esthetic quality.

It is important to note that this element of unity gives an experience a distinctive quality which pervades all the parts. It cannot be attributed to any one of the parts nor is it attained through the mere summation of them. It is there by virtue of the particular relationships which exist between them. A simple example may serve to illustrate this point. Let us take the sentence, "I bought a brown suit yesterday." This may be read or spoken as "I bought a *brown* suit yesterday." If, however, it is read "I bought a brown *suit* yesterday," the meaning of the sentence is considerably changed. Likewise, putting stress on any other one of the words in the sentence will result in another change in meaning. Thus, the meaning of the sentence inheres in the particular relationship existing between the words which form it. Furthermore, any one of the words, when placed in another sentence, will take on a new quality and meaning depending upon the new relationship in which it is placed. So too the quality of an experience inheres in the particular relationship

<hr>

[3] From *Art as Experience*, p. 35, by John Dewey. Copyright, 1936, by John Dewey. Courtesy G. P. Putnam's Sons.
[4] Herbert Read, *Education through Art* (New York: Pantheon Books, 1949), p. 35.

which binds the component parts together to form *an* experience. It is in the perception of this relationship that the esthetic character of experience resides. Dewey, in reference to intellectual experience, makes the following comments:

. . . the experience itself has a satisfying emotional quality because it possesses internal integration and fulfillment reached through ordered and organized movement. This artistic structure may be immediately felt. In so far, it is esthetic. What is even more important is that not only is this quality a significant motive in undertaking intellectual inquiry and in keeping it honest, but that no intellectual activity is an integral event (is *an* experience), unless it is rounded out with this quality.[5]

It appears from this statement that a purely intellectual understanding of the relationships in a situation is not sufficient for the perception of its esthetic quality. Intellectual comprehension by itself indicates only that the parts of the experience do have a coherent relationship and that this relationship gives meaning to the situation. But insofar as understanding of the situation is confined to intellectual comprehension, there is no esthetic experience. It is the presence of affective factors—an emotional response to the artistic structure of the situation—that lends an esthetic quality to the experience. In this connection, Dewey has written:

Physical things from far ends of the earth are physically transported and physically caused to act and react upon one another in the construction of a new object. The miracle of mind is that something similar takes place in experience without physical transport and assembling. Emotion is the moving and cementing force. It selects what is congruous and dyes what is selected with its color, thereby giving qualitative unity to materials externally disparate and dissimilar. It thus provides unity in and through the varied parts of an experience. When the unity is of the sort already described, the experience has esthetic character even though it is not, dominantly, an esthetic experience.[6]

Ogden is among the psychologists who have identified as esthetic the affective factors involved in perception of total situations or experiences:

[5] Dewey, *op. cit.*, p. 38.
[6] *Ibid.*, p. 42.

Long before we are able to think about life in general, and about its larger problems, we are guided in the pursuit of ends that are not comprised within the cycle of a single perception. And this guidance is afforded, not by discernment, but by *feeling*. In the discernment of a perceived event our disposition is a positive factor no less real than the event itself. The feelings which attach to a dispositional readiness for response—either in a single perception, or in a series of perceptions, interrupted, perchance, by pauses of sleep and distraction—are *aesthetic*. It is the aesthetic feelings that mark the rhythms of life, and hold us to our course by a kind of weight and balance. . . . A disposition to feel the completeness of an experienced event as being right and fit constitutes what we have called the aesthetic factor in perception.[7]

This quotation from Ogden emphasizes the intuitive character of esthetic response. Every individual has had the experience of learning some complex skill involving the coordination of a number of separate operations, such as swinging a baseball bat or bowing a violin. As the individual achieves mastery of the skill, he is aware of this mastery not so much because he has gained a greater intellectual understanding of the relation and synchronization of the separate movements; he recognizes it rather because a combination of sensory responses leads to an intuitive feeling of rightness. He knows that he is doing it correctly because it "feels" right. The efficiency of his performance—the hitting of the ball or the improved tone of the violin—provides a check on the correctness of his intuition.

It is clear that this concept of intuitive response bears a close relationship to the Gestalt concept of insight. The similarity is exemplified in a passage from Herbert Read's *Education through Art*. In commenting on the inadequacy of the word "intelligence" to describe the well-educated man, he speaks of a "wider concept—which includes sensibility and insight as well as intellect and reasoning, the perception of a pattern in relational cognition, and not merely the awareness of the discrete relations, the *raison sensitive* as well as the *raison intellectuelle*." [8] It is not within the scope of this study to argue the many differentiations which may be made between insight and intuition. There is

[7] Robert M. Ogden, *Psychology and Education* (New York: Harcourt, Brace and Co., 1932), pp. 112–13, 114.
[8] Read, *op. cit.*, p. 250.

enormous variation among the authorities as to the ways in which they define these two terms. Common to all the definitions of intuition, however, seems to be, first, the idea of response to a situation as a unified whole. Thus, Dewey, in defining intuition, speaks of ". . . the union of old and new, of foreground and background. . . ." [9] And Langer refers to ". . . that less known organ of intuition, imagination, whereby we perceive separate events, each under its own *Gestalt*. . . ." [10]

The second commonly recognized characteristic of the intuitive process is its affective quality. Gardner Murphy, in *Personality*, defines intuition as "doing what a human being does when he makes an integrated perceptual response to a very complex situation, no component of which reaches the level of a clear and reportable image." [11] Later in the same volume, he says, "If, instead of being approached by the geometrician or the carpenter in terms of the measuring rod, it [form] is pursued by the artist in terms of '*feeling for' the form he wants*, the response is properly called intuitive." [12]

From the above discussion it would appear that while an experience has esthetic quality by virtue of its dynamic unity the individual's response is esthetic only as it is an affective response. As he perceives the situation intuitively and with emotion, he perceives it esthetically. This may appear, at first sight, to discount the role of the intellect in esthetic perception. It seems clear, however, that emotional response is dependent upon cognition. If an individual does not understand an event or a situation he can respond only with indifference or bewilderment. Intellectual comprehension of the elements of a situation provides the basis for an integrated emotional reaction, but it is emotion which, as Dewey says, "is the moving and cementing force" and by virtue of which the individual can feel experience as a unified whole. In this connection, he has commented further as follows:

[9] Dewey, *op. cit.*, p. 266.
[10] Susanne K. Langer, "The Principles of Creation in Art," *The Hudson Review*, II (1949), 516.
[11] Gardner Murphy, *Personality: A Biosocial Approach to Origins and Structure* (New York: Harper and Brothers, 1947), p. 358.
[12] *Ibid.*, p. 359.

Only the psychology that has separated things which in reality belong together holds that scientists and philosophers think while poets and painters follow their feelings. In both, and to the same extent in the degree in which they are of comparable rank, there is emotionalized thinking, and there are feelings whose substance consists of appreciated meanings or ideas.[13]

DISTINCTIVE CHARACTERISTICS OF THE ART EXPERIENCE

If all experience, to the extent that it is unified and integrated, has esthetic quality—if, as Read says, life itself is possible only by virtue of an esthetic form or order—then we may reasonably ask what serves to distinguish a *distinctively* esthetic experience from *any* unified experience. On what basis may the appreciation of a Bach sonata be differentiated from the sense of pleasure which is experienced from the solution of a problem in calculus, or the enjoyment of a sunset from the enjoyment of a Van Gogh painting?

The answer appears to be in the purpose for which the activity is initiated and which controls its development and consummation. We may have an esthetic experience as we look at the sunset or perceive the relationships in a mathematical formula, but the esthetic quality, in these cases, is in the nature of a by-product. In the case of the mathematical formula, for example, its central purpose, its content, and its meaning lie elsewhere. The unified organization which lends it esthetic quality *looks toward* an end outside and beyond itself, is a means and not an end for its own sake. It is conceivable that the mathematician who constructs formulae for the sheer esthetic pleasure which he derives from their symmetry has converted mathematics into an art form. But this is not the usual case and the distinction indicated here is still a valid one, for the experience which is distinctively esthetic—that is, the art experience—has no meaning or purpose beyond the relationships by virtue of which the experience is a dynamic unity. A practical object—let us take, for example, a chair—must be judged in terms of its primary function, as a comfortable thing to sit in. Its formal relationships of legs to seat, seat to back, color and texture of wood and upholstery, are secondary considerations. The chair may

[13] Dewey, *op. cit.*, p. 73.

be offensive to the esthetic sense and still, in terms of its primary function alone, it may be a successful chair. Likewise, a chair of elegant proportion and line which is uncomfortable to sit in must be judged a poor chair. On the other hand, an object or event of purely esthetic interest is judged solely in terms of the extent to which it expresses unified and dynamic interrelationships. As MacMurray has said, ". . . the value of science is utility-value, while the value of art is intrinsic." [14] The purely artistic creation has no other purpose than the expression, in symbolic form, of dynamic relationships which have been perceived and found meaningful through intuitive and emotional processes.

MacMurray has shown that the essence of artistic creation is the personal, the emotional, and the intuitive. He develops his argument by means of the analogy of two people engaged in a conversation. If the two people are intimate friends, their conversation about a thing or an event is not merely an exchange of information; it is also a means whereby each reveals himself to the other. The event about which they talk together may have no particular significance in itself; it may, in fact, be quite trivial. It derives its significance from the fact that it is the means whereby the two people are related to each other. If, on the other hand, they have no personal interest in each other, the conversation is no longer a means of self-communication.

Each separately is interested in the thing discussed for its own sake, and not at all for the sake of the other person's interest in it, so that the total significance of the speech-situation resides, for the persons concerned, in the object. Thus the object, the third person, becomes the essence of the situation, and the conversation becomes a matter of giving and receiving information about it. The full speech-situation has been degraded to an impersonal level, and at that level the experience is no longer emotional, but merely intellectual. . . .

Science, in the full sense, is the systematic development to universality of this information-giving and information-receiving attitude in personal relations.[15]

[14] John MacMurray, *Reason and Emotion*, p. 155. Copyright, 1938, D. Appleton-Century Company, Inc.
[15] *Ibid.*, pp. 149–50.

In continuing the discussion, MacMurray has us imagine one friend telling another about his intensely personal reactions to a winter sunset in the Alps.

This is no scientific description; dispensed, labelled and docketed information; but information clothed in the flesh of imagery and pulsing with the blood of emotion—a communication of self. Now imagine that in the telling he becomes so wrapped and thrilled in his experience that he becomes indifferent to the personality of his listener; that the friend becomes just somebody—anybody—to whom he can express himself about the marvel of that night at Mürren; then he has become the artist and his talk is the essence of art.[16]

It is important to remember at this point that artistic creation is not merely an outpouring of emotion. If this were so, there would be no way of distinguishing essentially between the scream of an angry child and a Botticelli Venus. By the same token, if Michelangelo had been actually experiencing the horrors of the damned when he painted "The Last Judgment," he would have been completely incapable of articulate expression. The art object is not a direct expression of raw emotion; rather it is the expression, or symbolization, of relationships which are emotionally significant and which have been so perceived by the creator.

There is one further question which requires clarification. This has to do with the so-called "useful" arts. If the meaning and purpose of the esthetic object resides solely in the symbolization of emotionally significant relationships, then it would appear that the term "useful arts" is a contradiction in terms. "Useful" implies that there is some utility value in an object, and it has already been stated that the value of art is intrinsic, that it has no end beyond itself. How, then, can an object be useful and, at the same time, be an object of esthetic interest?

F. S. C. Northrop, in *The Meeting of East and West*, refers to "art in its first function, and art in its second function." He amplifies this distinction as follows:

Art in its first function is to be defined as art, such as that exemplified in Georgia O'Keeffe's "Abstraction" . . . which uses the im-

[16] *Ibid.*, p. 153.

mediately apprehended aesthetic materials of the differentiated aesthetic continuum to convey those materials and that continuum in and for themselves and for their own sake. Art in its second function, on the other hand, by the use of theoretically controlled and defined techniques such as perspective, uses the aesthetic materials and the aesthetic continuum not merely in and for themselves for their own sake, but also analogically and symbolically to convey the theoretic component of the nature of things of which they are the mere correlate or sign.[17]

The theoretic component of which Northrop speaks may be equated with what has been referred to here as the scientific and the utilitarian. Elsewhere in the same work, Northrop refers to a "spectrum of aesthetic possibilities." In explaining this concept he writes:

The beauty of an abstract, analytical, mathematical proof, because of the large amount of the formal and theoretical, and the minimum amount of the intuitive and the ineffable in its content, stands very near the extreme purely theoretic end of the aesthetic spectrum; just as a painting like Georgia O'Keeffe's Abstraction No. 3 . . . into which it is difficult to read an inferred theoretic reference stands near the other extreme, purely aesthetic, end of the spectrum. In between the two extremes are to be located all the actual art of the past and the potential art of the present and future. . . .[18]

The answer seems to be that we may apply, in varying degrees, criteria both of utility and of esthetic interest to the same object. The relative weight of these criteria may vary from one period to another with respect to certain objects or events, from one individual to another, or within a single individual. It seems safe to assume, for example, that many of the implements and artifacts made by primitive people were regarded by them primarily as objects of use and were so judged. While primitive craftsmen may have been quite aware of the artistry involved in making weapons or vessels, this was probably secondary in importance to the mechanical efficiency of the products. Today, such fine examples as have found their way into museums are not valued by us because they are efficient knives or containers for grain or oil, but because they are objects of esthetic enjoyment.

[17] F. S. C. Northrop, *The Meeting of East and West* (New York: The Macmillan Company, 1946), p. 306.
[18] *Ibid.*, p. 490.

We do not judge them in terms of utility since for us they are not useful objects and whatever value they still have is esthetic value. To take another example, an individual who is extremely sensitive may make some concessions with respect to his comfort in order that the furniture in his house shall satisfy his esthetic requirements, while another individual will reject the same furniture because his values are more heavily weighted in terms of comfort and utility. Thus it may be seen that esthetic sensitivity, or the lack of it, will influence value judgments in areas of living which themselves are not purely esthetic.

However, it should be pointed out that these two standards of value need not always stand in opposition to each other. · On the contrary, they may enhance each other. A comfortable chair may be more enjoyable because it is a thing of beauty, and its beauty will be more highly prized because it serves a practical end. It is this happy union of beauty and utility which is the aim of the useful arts. The principle which has been most widely acclaimed in the visual arts that form follows function is a useful one and has been most salutary in its effect on contemporary art; but by itself it is not enough. Function unquestionably sets limits on the form which an object may take; but if it is defined merely in terms of physical and mechanical efficiency it will be a problem solely for the scientist and the engineer. In light of the distinction made earlier, the resulting object may have esthetic quality by virtue of its formal relationships, just as a mathematical formula has esthetic quality. But only as it has been consciously designed as a symbol of emotionally significant relationships will it be a distinctively artistic object.

ART AND CREATIVITY

It follows logically from the foregoing discussion that art activity, to the extent that it is honest, is essentially creative. This is so because it depends, first and foremost, upon the personal factor. As MacMurray points out, to the extent that activity becomes impersonal, it partakes of the nature of science. Art activity, on the other hand, springs from the inner life of the individual. Because every individual is unique, his inner life, his life of emotion and feeling, is unlike anyone else's. Thus, to the extent that he has integrity of purpose and honesty of expression, the relationships which he builds out of his emotional life will be original and creative.

It is necessary here to digress from the main argument long enough to point out that creative activity and art activity are by no means synonymous. Any activity which is genuinely artistic is necessarily creative, but a creative approach may be applied to any kind of a problem. The invention of the cotton gin and the development of the atomic bomb were as truly creative as was the production of Beethoven's Ninth Symphony or Picasso's "Guernica"; and, as has already been shown, they have esthetic quality in the degree that they are configurations of dynamically interrelated parts, but they are certainly not creations of the artistic imagination.

We may go one step further and say that creativity does not necessarily lead to desirable ends. The development of atomic energy has enormous potentialities either for good or for evil. Again, the methods used by a bank robber or a murderer may be highly original and ingenious, and, in a very real sense, creative, but the purposes to which he has lent his creativity are judged by society as undesirable. By the same token, propaganda art, whether its purpose be to convince its audience of the superiority of a certain kind of tooth paste or to convert them to a particular social ideology, while it may be most artfully contrived and give evidence of creative skill on the part of its originator, must be judged from the standpoint of its social value as well as its artistic value. To the extent that creative ability is directed toward utilitarian purposes it invites judgment in terms of social values.

The idea of creativeness is frequently associated with, and limited to, the idea of genius. The argument back of this concept of creativity is that no achievement is genuinely creative unless it is new in the experience of society and only genius is capable of such achievement. As it is used in the present discussion, however, the word denotes independent activity on the part of any individual which is motivated by his own intelligence and his emotional and intuitive response to living situations, and which, therefore, results in the origination of patterns that are new in his own experience. Defined in this way, creativeness lies within the potentialities of all individuals and is not a "special" ability in the sense that some have it and others do not. Gardner Murphy has written:

We know from watching children in progressive schools that the desire to create must be almost universal, and that almost everyone has some measure of originality which stems from his fresh perception of life and experience, and from the uniqueness of his own fantasy when he is free to share it.[19]

It is abundantly clear, however, that there is enormous variation among individuals in their ability and their disposition to act creatively. At one extreme we find the individual who accepts and depends upon the word of others in the solution of all his problems and is utterly at sea when faced with the necessity of independent action. At the other extreme we find the creative genius who makes it his way of life to explore new areas of experience. It is of the utmost importance for education that we know the sources of this variation.

Murphy has written that "the first great phase in the evolution of the creator appears to be extreme *sensitiveness* to a specific form of experience, usually sensory; it is especially likely to involve sight, sound, or the muscle sense. It embodies delight in these experiences, a need for more of them, a curiosity into their relationships. . . . in other words we are dealing with sensory and activity drives. . . . Creativeness begins with impressions, sensitivities, wants, energies." [20] With specific reference to artistic creativity, MacMurray has written:

He [the artist] is emotionally contemplative. He fills his senses with an object or a set of objects, and seeks to feel it; to become emotionally aware of its being, and to realize it fully as that individual thing. That is his attitude to the world, when he is being an artist. He wants to go out to it, to soak himself in it and so to become emotionally conscious of its meaning and significance in itself. He is not trying to discover things about it but to know it as something that exists in its own right, something that is part of the furniture of earth, and therefore has its value in itself—not for him or for anyone else. His success depends entirely upon his

[19] Murphy, *op. cit.*, p. 453.
[20] *Ibid.*, p. 452.

ability to get outside himself, as it were—to lose himself in what he sees, and to feel its nature and its life. So far as he can do this he finds that it has the result of producing in him a spontaneous creative activity which expresses the awareness of the thing which he has achieved. If he paints a picture, what the picture says is not 'This is what the object looks like; so, if you have seen this you needn't look at the object'; it says rather: 'I have known something—really known it—and this is what it means in itself. Look at this and you will realize the significance of the thing as it revealed itself to me.' [21]

If we return for a moment to the earlier discussion of the nature of esthetic experience, it will be remembered that the following ideas were proposed: first, that any experience (and therefore any activity) has esthetic quality to the extent that it has dynamic unity; second, that the appreciation of this quality depends, not upon intellectual comprehension, but upon affective factors of intuition and emotion; and third, that an experience or activity is distinctively esthetic to the extent that those intuitively perceived relationships are regarded as ends which are sufficient in themselves. It follows logically from these propositions that all creative activity, to the extent that it results in the consummation of a complete act, has esthetic quality. The purpose of this recapitulation is to show the striking relationship which these ideas bear to the two quotations cited above. Murphy has stated that creativity depends upon sensitiveness to one's environment and experiences. He has not specified, however, whether the individual responds to an experience as something to be relished on its own merits or as a means to some other end. Indeed, he states subsequently, by way of example, that "the delight of watching the panorama of personal life may fuse with the delight of achieving power over people and of receiving recognition or applause from them, until one becomes a miniature statesman in his neighborhood or boy's club or fraternity, and goes on to a diplomatic or parliamentary career." [22] This clearly is a kind of creative activity which is not distinctively esthetic; it proceeds from a sensitivity to relationships as means rather than as ends in themselves.

By contrast, the artist who is described by MacMurray is

[21] MacMurray, *op. cit.,* p. 59.
[22] Murphy, *op. cit.,* p. 455.

sensitive to a thing or an event "as something that exists in its own right . . . and therefore has value in itself. . . ." This provides the parallel to the distinctively esthetic experience which has no purpose beyond the dynamic unity which it presents and by virtue of which it exists. The artist—that is, any person behaving with artistic motivation—values his sensitivity for the revelation of new experiences which have intrinsic value for the enrichment of his living.

There are at least three factors which are responsible for the differences individuals exhibit in kind and degree of sensitivity. The first of these is native endowment. We know, for example, that individuals vary greatly in sensory acuity, and this alone would be sufficient to explain great diversity and variation in sensitivity. If we add to this the capacities necessary for a sensitive appreciation of such complex experiences as are involved in human relationships, the possible range in sensitivity is increased still further. A second factor has to do with the richness and the variety of the environment in which the individual lives. Quite aside from considerations of native endowment, the child who goes to work in a cotton mill at the age of twelve has only a fraction of the opportunities for sensitive response that are open to a child who has the freedom of life on a farm or in a school that provides rich and varied experiences. The third factor relates to the culture in which the individual lives. The culture itself may either encourage or inhibit sensitivity and spontaneity of response. As Murphy has stated, "Society gives appreciation, status, and a role to the potentially creative individual; or it may fail to give them, in which case potential creativeness withers at the root." [23]

A second factor which is necessary for creative activity is what Murphy has called "a pattern of creative skills." [24] He points out that "One may, like Sidney Lanier, swoon at the beauty of the music of the violin but see or hear nothing articulate enough to record." [25] After some discussion, he concludes that "Since skill of this sort is doubtless dependent on general

[23] *Ibid.*, p. 454.
[24] *Ibid.*, p. 456.
[25] *Loc. cit.*

intelligence and on various special abilities, we shall content ourselves with the banal statement that an intellectual feature must be added to the affective factor." [26] This statement forces us to the conclusion that Lanier did not have the necessary intellectual capacity to master the complexities of musical performance or composition. This explanation, therefore, seems hardly adequate. It seems more likely that the pattern of creative skills is closely related to an imaginative capacity which enables the individual to see in given data the possibilities for new relationships. This, it would seem, is as closely allied to intuition and feeling as to pure intellect. It is the ability to "feel" the rightness of a pictorial composition or the proper bowing of a violin string. Of equal importance is the disposition and eagerness to experiment, to seek, through deliberate manipulation of elements, new patterns and relationships. Only in the rarest cases is the creative product born full-fledged in the mind of the creator. It comes to full life through a painful process of experimentation, trials, errors, and new trials. It is necessary to conclude, therefore, that although intelligence is unquestionably necessary in creative activity, as it is in any goal-directed activity, to it must be added a factor of imagination which can envisage new relationships, and a capacity for experimentation.

In *The Mind of the Maker*, Dorothy Sayers, while speaking in less scientific terms, seems to deal more adequately with this pattern of creative skills when she postulates a creative "trinity" of Idea, Energy, and Power.[27] The Creative Idea may be equated with creative imagination, the ability to envisage new possibilities and new relationships, for she says, "The word is here used . . . quite simply in the sense intended by the writer when he says: 'I have an idea for a book.' " [28] Creative Energy is the activity of the creator through which the Idea takes on material form, and this involves skill in the handling of the medium in which he is working, mastery of his technique. Creative Power is "the meaning of the work and its response in the

[26] *Loc. cit.*
[27] Dorothy Sayers, *The Mind of the Maker* (New York: Harcourt, Brace and Co., 1941), pp. 37 ff.
[28] *Ibid.*, p. 38.

lively soul. . . ." [29] This, it would appear, is closely related to a receptivity on the part of the individual which renders him sensitive to his environment and also to his creation as an emotionally significant event.

It is important to note that no one of these factors is sufficient in itself, and only as the three of them are united and work in and through each other can creative activity proceed. Emphasis on the Idea, without the support of Energy and Power, produces "the man who 'has the most marvellous idea for a book, if only he had the time to sit down and write it.' " [30] An excess of Energy produces "the prestidigitators of verbal arabesque and rime leonine; the alembicated, the pretentious, and the precious, and those who (like Meredith at his worst) wrap up the commonplace in tortuous complexities—all those, in fact, whose manner has degenerated into mannerism." [31] The individual ridden by Power (or by emotional excess) "conceives that the emotion which he feels is in itself sufficient to awaken response, without undergoing discipline of a thorough incarnation, and without the coherence that derives from reference to a controlling idea. Such a man may write with the tears streaming down his cheeks, and yet produce nothing but turgid rhetoric, flat insipidity, or the absurdities of an Amanda Ros." [32]

Creative activity in the arts, therefore, seems to involve a complex of closely related factors. There must, first of all, be a degree of sensitivity to the environment, a responsiveness to the experiences of living. But sensitivity alone produces our Sidney Laniers. In addition to emotional receptivity and awareness, the individual must possess an imaginative capacity which enables him to organize his responses into new and emotionally significant patterns and relationships—the ability to originate a "controlling idea" or a *Gestalt* out of the miscellany of his impressions and responses. And finally, if the creative idea is to be given material form—is to become a work of art, in other words—there must be skill in handling the techniques and the materials of the artistic medium.

[29] *Ibid.*, pp. 37–38.
[30] *Ibid.*, p. 151.
[31] *Ibid.*, p. 152.
[32] *Ibid.*, p. 154.

ART EXPERIENCE AND PERSONAL GROWTH

In the foregoing discussion, the attempt has been made to show how art experience is related to the entire span of the individual's experience, what its distinctive characteristics are, and whence it arises. It may still be justly asked to what end it contributes. Granted that it has a given relationship to human experience, what are its values in terms of individual human living? Does it, indeed, represent a valid and desirable goal?

THE VALIDITY OF ESTHETIC EXPERIENCE

In a culture such as ours, which regards the cultivation of the intellect as the supreme goal of human endeavor, any favorable reference to the life of emotion is apt to be regarded with suspicion. As Bigelow has pointed out, we tend to believe that our emotions are not to be trusted and that we are most rational when we are least emotional.[33] In *The Meeting of East and West*, F. S. C. Northrop has developed the thesis that this relative evaluation of the scientific-intellectual aspect of reality as opposed to its esthetic-emotional aspect has been the dominant influence in directing the development of Western culture.[34] He proceeds from the idea that reality—man and his environment—is composed of two factors or components: the theoretic component and the esthetic component. Whereas Western culture has concerned itself primarily with the theoretic component, the culture of the Oriental world has been largely preoccupied with the esthetic component. The basic difference in approach to the realities of living, says Northrop, is at the root of the great social conflicts which characterize the contemporary world.

Northrop pursues his argument in terms of large cultural patterns and their characteristic ideological doctrines. Since these large patterns have their source in the minds of individual men, we may ask, regarding our Western culture, how the preoccupation with scientific reality has affected the development of the

[33] Karl W. Bigelow, "The Challenge of Art in a Time of Crisis," *Art Education in a Free Society*, 1947 Yearbook of the Eastern Arts Association (Kutztown: The Association, 1947), p. 40.
[34] Northrop, *op. cit.*, pp. 300 ff.

individual. In *The Grass Roots of Art*, Herbert Read deals with this question in the following manner:

We have never dared to trace the connections between the disordered state of our civilization and our traditional systems of education. If our schools were producing naturally and normally personalities which we could describe as balanced, integrated or harmonious, we should not be able to tolerate a condition of universal disunity and mutual distrust. We should therefore re-examine our whole tradition of education since the Renaissance and dare to ask ourselves whether it has been generally productive of individual serenity and social harmony. We might then have to confess that in our exclusive preoccupation with knowledge and science, we had omitted to educate those human faculties which are connected with the emotional and integrative aspects of human life—that we had carefully nurtured inhuman monsters, with certain organs of the intelligence gigantically enlarged, others completely atrophied.[85]

As Read clearly indicates, there is no place in the world of science for emotion and feeling; only as we eliminate them are we able to approach scientific truth. Science is in pursuit of facts—facts which are the same for everyone and are independent of personal reaction and emotion. Thus, as MacMurray says, "As soon as the scientist is disturbed by a strong emotion, his work is deranged; he ceases to be scientific and becomes a human being."[36] Because our culture is so strongly dominated by a scientific orientation and we are so preoccupied with the search for scientific fact, we have come to the point where we regard emotion as inappropriate to any sphere of activity. What has happened, therefore, in terms of individual human living, is a choking off, a repression, of the life of emotion and feeling. In our neglect of the esthetic-emotional component of reality, we have failed almost completely to develop this vital area of human experience and expression. We have, in fact, gone to some pains to discourage it and it has survived only because human living depends upon its survival. The necessary relationship between emotion and intellect has been disregarded, and we have failed to understand that only through a fusion of the

[85] Herbert Read, *The Grass Roots of Art* (New York: Wittenborn, Schultz Inc., 1949), p. 64.
[86] MacMurray, *op. cit.*, p. 150.

two can we experience life fully. Moholy-Nagy describes this relationship in the following quotation:

Theoretically, man is the sum total of his psycho-physical, intellectual, and emotional potentialities. His reasoning power parallels the emotional forces. What he knows, he could also feel if he would train himself in both spheres. In fact, this is his historic struggle, to arrive at an integrated life in which he would function to the fullest of his capacities through a synthesis of the intellectual and the emotional, through the coordination of penetrative thinking and profound feeling. To reach this goal—to feel what we know and know what we feel—is one of the tasks of our generation.[37]

In other words, if man is to experience life fully, he must achieve a balance between the theoretic and the esthetic, between intellect and emotion. Indeed, according to MacMurray, emotion and intellect are not to be regarded as two equal and complementary aspects of a full life; rather intellect is the means whereby the full and free play of emotion may be more completely realized as the desirable end of living:

The emotional life is not simply a part or an aspect of human life. It is not, as we so often think, subordinate, or subsidiary to the mind. It is the core and essence of human life. The intellect arises out of it, is rooted in it, draws its nourishment and sustenance from it, and is the subordinate partner in the human economy. This is because the intellect is essentially instrumental. Thinking is not living. At its worst it is a substitute for living; at its best a means of living better. . . . the emotional life is our life, both as awareness of the world and as action in the world, so far as it is lived for its own sake. Its value lies in itself, not in anything beyond it which it is a means of achieving.[38]

Traditional education, to the extent that it has been concerned with the emotions, has regarded them largely as impediments to well-ordered living. Development of the intellect, which, as MacMurray says, should be properly regarded as a means, has been conceived as the highest end of education and of life. In one sense only has it been regarded as instrumental, that through it the emotions might be controlled, held in check, and prevented from interfering with our objective contemplation of the world.

[37] L. Moholy-Nagy, *Vision in Motion* (Chicago: Paul Theobald, 1947), pp. 10–11.
[38] MacMurray, *op. cit.*, p. 75.

But this objective contemplation must now be seen itself as a means—a means to fuller experiencing and fuller savoring of the world through our emotions and our feelings. In order to clarify the relevance of this point of view to the present discussion, it is necessary to indicate more specifically the contributions which art experience makes to the life of emotion.

REFINEMENT OF EMOTIONAL AND INTUITIVE PERCEPTIONS

It is a commonly accepted idea that our emotions are the irrational part of our nature and that they can be disciplined only as they are subordinated to the intellect. It is only through logical processes of thinking that we can discover what is right and what is wrong, what is good and what is evil. Having discovered this, we then apply the appropriate controls to our emotions, suppressing them where they are in conflict with known facts, and this with only indifferent success. One of the clichés of our culture is the statement, "I know it's wrong, but that's the way I feel." The assumption underlying this statement is that our feelings are what they are and there's precious little we can do about changing them.

MacMurray has shown that, in reality, the mind is capable only of collecting and observing the facts about a situation and that judgments of right and wrong—in fact, all the motivations of human action—are the function of the emotions.[39] It is true that knowledge of the facts *about* a situation will furnish us guides for our value judgments and must, therefore, be fully explored. But in addition to knowing *about* a situation intellectually, we must also know it emotionally, must be able to feel it.

There can be faulty feeling just as surely as there can be faulty thinking. To feel an unreasoning hate for all men whose skin is black, for example, is as wrong as to think that two times two is five. Both of them are wrong because they do not correspond with the realities of the situations with which they deal. Just as thinking is correct to the degree that it corresponds to realities of fact, so feeling is correct insofar as it corresponds to the realities of the affectively perceived world. And just as rational

[39] *Ibid.*, pp. 23–24.

thinking depends upon fully experiencing the world of fact, so rational feeling depends upon fully experiencing the world of sense and emotion. It is precisely at this point that esthetic experience is of the utmost importance.

Edman has written that ". . . the basis and the ultimate appeal of all art is sensuous." In amplifying this point, he says:

We become engaged, as it were, by the amiable and intensified surfaces of things. The charm of a still life is certainly in its composition, but it is the blues and greens and yellows of the fruit that arrest us; our body becomes alive to what the senses present. Those moralists who have regarded art as a sensuous distraction have sourly stated the truth. Eyes dulled and routinated have become keen again in the observation of painting; the ear becomes a subtilized organ of precise and intense sensation. We move in painting and in music not among the abstract possibilities of action but among the concrete actualities of what is there to be seen and heard.[40]

Edman continues his discussion as follows:

The arts do more, however, than simply intensify sensations. In the routine of our lives, successively similar situations have produced successively similar emotional reactions. We become dulled emotionally as well as sensuously. In the clear and artful discipline of a novel or a drama our emotions become reinstated into a kind of pure intensity. It might appear on the surface that the actualities of life, the impingements of those so very real crises of birth and death and love, are more intense than any form of art provides. That is true. But we do not live always amid crises, and the ordinary run of our experiences gives us only emotions that are dull and thin. A tragedy like *Hamlet*, a novel like *Anna Karenina*, clarify and deepen for us emotional incidents of familiar human situations. For many people, it is literature rather than life that teaches them what their native emotions are. And ideas themselves, which in the abstractions of formal reasoning may be thin and cold and external, in the passionate presentation of poetry and drama may become intimate and alive.[41]

Art, therefore, or, more broadly speaking, the esthetic attitude, provides the means whereby the individual may experience the world more fully through his senses and his emotions, for to

[40] Irwin Edman, *Arts and the Man* (New York: W. W. Norton and Co., 1939), pp. 28–29.
[41] *Ibid.*, pp. 29–30.

do this is, in truth, to have an esthetic attitude. By means of esthetic perception he achieves a greater measure of sensitivity and intensity in his living and thus gains an ever greater maturity of emotion and intuition.

ACHIEVING NEW UNDERSTANDINGS THROUGH ESTHETIC PERCEPTION

Through such direct sensuous and emotional experience, the individual not only heightens and refines his capacities for perception but also gains access to new ways of perceiving and understanding his environment. Let us take a simple example. An individual who operates entirely in terms of utility values will see in wood a very efficient and adaptable material for building houses and barns, and for making furniture and implements. If he has any scientific knowledge of woods, he will know that some are stronger than others, some more adaptable to one purpose than to another. This is one way of knowing about wood, and all this can be known without ever having seen a piece of it. To actually know the substance itself requires that he must have had the experience of running his hand over a finely finished wood surface, of feeling the lightness of redwood and the weight of maple, of seeing the pattern in quarter-sawed walnut, of smelling a piece of lignum vitae, and of watching a birch rod bend under the weight of his hands. This is not just more scientific knowledge; it is knowledge of a new kind, understanding of different dimensions.

Similarly, during the Spanish Civil War we may have read many newspaper accounts of the siege of Guernica. We may, indeed, have had emotional reactions of some intensity. But seeing Picasso's Guernica mural gives us new insights and new understandings because it is not a reportorial statement of the facts of the siege of Guernica. It is an intense symbolic expression of Picasso's emotional apprehension of this event. He is telling us, not what he *knows* but what he *feels* about Guernica. Factual information about this tragic event would be the same from any source so long as it was a reliable source. But only from this painting can we get the particular meanings which were significant to the painter. Therefore, to the extent that we are able to apprehend the painting, we have enriched our own store of meanings.

Anyone who has seen the Guernica mural knows that it is not an entirely pleasurable experience and, on this ground, may object to it as being "inartistic." Indeed, it is a widely held theory that all esthetic experience must be pleasurable and that the value of art is in the escape it provides from the distressing realities of an imperfect world. The arts may certainly function in this way in many instances. But to state this as their sole function is to misunderstand the relation of the arts to living. They are not a prettification, but rather, an intensification of living, and they draw upon the entire range of human experience. A more intense perception of pleasure brings with it a more intense perception of pain. As MacMurray has written:

> We must choose between a life that is thin and narrow, uncreative and mechanical, with the assurance that even if it is not very exciting it will not be intolerably painful; and a life in which the increase in its fullness and creativeness brings a vast increase in delight, but also in pain and hurt. . . . If we choose to minimize pain we must damp down human sensitiveness, and so limit the sources of possible delight. If we decide to increase our joy in life we can only do it by accepting a heightened sensitiveness to pain.[42]

The rewards of esthetic perception are not a mere titillation of our capacities for pleasurable sensation and emotion. They are a more intense and complete apprehension of the totality of experience. One artist may incline toward a happier kind of artistic statement than another; this may be seen by a comparison of the compositions of Mendelssohn and Tchaikowsky, for example. But on this basis one composer cannot be judged superior to the other, or his mode of expression more valid. In this respect, each has equal validity and each can give us new meanings and new insights into experience.

The word "insights" is used advisedly here for it points up a significant aspect of esthetic experience, that it illuminates understanding not only by increasing our store of emotionally significant meanings but also by leading toward a fuller integration of meanings. While this follows inescapably from

[42] MacMurray, *op. cit.*, p. 47.

arguments presented earlier, it seems worth while to point it out specifically. It will be remembered that esthetic perception was described as the perception of emotionally significant *relationships*. If it were perception of isolated fragments of sensation or emotion there would be no building, no relating, no integration. But because relationships are the essence of the esthetic structure, there is more than a mere accumulation or aggregation. Implicit in the definition of esthetic perception which has been offered is the idea of constantly expanding patterns of dynamically interrelated meanings.

ART ACTIVITY AS THE EXPRESSION OF FELT MEANINGS

The preceding discussion has made explicit the idea that a work of art is basically the expression of felt meanings. No further discussion of that point is necessary here. However, the emphasis thus far has been primarily on esthetic perception as it contributes to the life of the individual. It is necessary, therefore, to deal more specifically with artistic expression as a process whereby the individual increases his understandings and insights.

Because all experience is interaction between organism and environment it represents a balance of what Dewey has called doing and undergoing.[43] An object or event is truly perceived only when the individual relates it to, and builds it into, his total fund of experiences. The extent to which an experience is integrated and meaningful depends not only upon the individual's receptivity but also upon his continual reconstruction of his experiences into larger wholes. This is a positive act and without it he is like a pond which ripples when a pebble is dropped into it and then returns to its former state of quiet.

We tend frequently to think of perception as all undergoing and expression as all doing. It may be seen, however, that this clear-cut distinction does not hold up, because just as perception involves doing so expression is impossible without undergoing. The expression of any feeling or emotion must always be in reference to something which has been undergone. When an individual expresses anger, for example, he is angry at something which has happened to him or been done to him.

[43] Dewey, *op. cit.*, pp. 44 ff.

The cry of rage or the tears of bitter disappointment, however, are not artistic expressions, and it is in the recognition of this fact that theories of art as *self-expression* have been attacked, for, as Langer has pointed out, "Sheer self-expression requires no artistic form." She continues:

A lynching-party howling round the gallows tree, a woman wringing her hands over a sick child, a lover who has just rescued his sweetheart in an accident and stands trembling, sweating, and perhaps laughing or crying with emotion, is giving vent to intense feelings; but such scenes are not occasions for music, least of all, for composing.[44]

And yet it must be acknowledged that the artist does express himself, else there is no way of explaining the great difference in personal styles between Salvador Dali and Thomas Hart Benton, or between George Gershwin and Aaron Copland. If the aim of these artists is not self-expression, then how can it be explained that each of them does express himself in a style that is highly personal and individual and that is clearly and unmistakably his own? And why, in all the arts, is there such emphasis on the development of an individual style of expression? Buermeyer provides an answer to these questions in the following passages:

An individual . . . expresses his personal individuality in the individuality of his world. . . . *He does not luxuriate in his own feelings*, but seeks and discovers that view or comprehension of things in which his feelings have their proper embodiment or expression. In so far as the world which his feelings grasp is a human world, it recognizes the quality of his feelings by his success in understanding *it*. . . .

. . . the greatest artist is the most impersonal artist. Of course, he is also the most personal. But his personality has passed into his world, and he shows himself in showing it. The greater artist always communicates his feeling by bringing out what is in his subject; the lesser, by adding to it what amounts to a gesture or exclamation of his own. A novelist who audibly sighs over or commends his characters makes us cold to them and cold to him.[45]

[44] Susanne K. Langer, *Philosophy in a New Key* (Cambridge: Harvard University Press, 1942), p. 216.
[45] Laurence Buermeyer, *Aesthetic Experience* (Merion: The Barnes Foundation Press, 1929), pp. 183–84. Italics the present author's.

The essence of artistic expression, therefore, is not a mere out-pouring of emotion, but an exploration and a fuller understanding of the world of experience in emotionally significant terms. The artistic product is self-expressive in the degree that the individual is a unique total personality for it will bear the stamp of his unique perception of the world. But his orientation is toward the things perceived, not toward his emotional reactions *per se.* Insofar as he responds with his total personality and is honest in his responses, the artistic product will be expressive of his personality. Buermeyer has written:

It is his *full* self that is unique, his full self molded by all that he has done and undergone, and not driven by any single impulse, with its partial and one-sided view of things; and the coordination of all his powers, the expression of his total self, is the same thing as the interpretation of an object in terms of all its relationships.[46]

What, then, are the values of artistic expression for the personal growth and development of the individual? In the first place, it provides the means whereby the individual can achieve a fuller and deeper understanding of the world. In order to express clearly it is necessary to perceive clearly, and thus the urge to express leads to closer attention to the clarification of meanings and the emergence of new understandings and new relationships. An experience, although but dimly understood, may have such powerful emotional significance as to motivate expression. To achieve clarity of expression, the individual must probe his experience more deeply, feel it more deeply. His own store of meanings is thereby enriched in both variety and intensity.

As he achieves a fuller understanding of the world, he also achieves a fuller understanding of himself, which is another way of saying that he achieves a more integrated personality. As Buermeyer has pointed out in the quotation above, the coordination of all the individual's powers is the same thing as the interpretation of an object in terms of all its relationships. Because his preoccupation is with emotionally significant relationships, the understanding for which he strives is in terms of his connec-

---

[46] *Ibid.,* p. 182.

tion with the object or experience and the nature of the interaction between it and him. Understanding of the self, therefore, is both a necessary condition for, and a result of, understanding the experience.

It may be objected that the best way to learn about life is to live it, and that the vicarious experiences of artistic activity are, at best, "warmed over" imitations of actual living experience. It is certainly true that there is no substitute for a full and rich life, but such an argument arises out of a misunderstanding of the nature of artistic activity. The art experience is not a negation of life experiences or an escape from them; rather, it is a distillation, an intensification, of the events of living. The distractions and the accidents of practical life, and the preoccupation of the individual with practical ends, are such as to blur and disfigure the significance of much of our experience. Irrelevancies intrude and concentration on the end toward which an experience is directed diverts our view from the experience itself. In this connection, Buermeyer has written as follows:

Art is to the life of feeling what the laboratory is to science, a place from which distracting factors may be excluded, and things so controlled as to reveal their maximum significance. And as laboratory experimentation is most enlightening and fruitful when it is most able to reproduce the conditions under which actual phenomena occur, so art is at its best when the imagination succeeds in illuminating and transfiguring most of what "men live by." [47]

Coomaraswamy has said that the artist is not a special kind of man but that every man is a special kind of artist.[48] This is not to say that every individual is equally endowed in his capacities for esthetic perception and expression. Rather, the emphasis must be on the fact that every individual does have the capacity, as well as the need, for esthetic experience. To the extent that this capacity is stifled or allowed to atrophy we are depriving the individual of a vital area of human living. The story is told of an exchange between the painter Turner and a lady who was looking at one of his paintings. With some impatience, she said to him, "Mr. Turner, I never saw a sunset like that." The painter

[47] Ibid., pp. 83-84.
[48] Quoted in Eric Gill, Art (London: John Lane, 1934), p. 6.

replied, "But don't you wish you could?" The arts, as Edman has said, ". . . show, in the literal sense of showing forth or presenting, possibilities of form in our experience and generate a love for order, clarity, and coherence, not as a cold intellectual ascent, but as a warm and intimate realization." [49]

It is equally important that each of us has not only the capacity for feeling but an urge to communicate to our fellow men those aspects of our experience that we find emotionally significant. It is the unique contribution of the arts to living that they are the vehicle through which this capacity can be developed and refined, for the arts offer a means for the expression of emotion and feeling which can be articulated in no other way. To neglect this area of living means, first, to block the channels for the expression of a natural human urge and, eventually, to bring on the atrophy of the urge itself—to hasten the growth of Read's "inhuman monsters." In the words of Edman, "The creation of art is the self-discipline of free minds. Its order is that of individuals at once vital and self-harmonied. In art are instances, more winning than argument, of what free society may achieve." [50]

[49] From an unpublished manuscript of a lecture delivered by Irwin Edman to the Committee on Art Education, May, 1950.
[50] *Loc. cit.*

Chapter V

ART AND SOCIETY

While the esthetic impulse is an affair of individual human beings, it also has social roots and social implications. It is almost universally recognized that the arts provide an unparalleled source of information with respect to the patterns and values of a culture, for they reveal not only the thoughts and feelings of individual artists but also the thoughts and feelings of the groups from which these artists have drawn their sustenance and strength. At the same time there is recognition of the enormous power which the arts have exerted in shaping the thought and the lives of the people in past cultures. It was recognition of this fact that led the Nazis in Germany to condemn modern art as "degenerate." Similarly, the arts provide the Communists with one of their most valuable instruments of propaganda for adherence to their particular social ideology.

Benedict has shown that in the study of cultures it has been impossible to discover any one system of relationships by which various traits are interwoven to form the cultural complex.[1]

[1] Ruth Benedict, *Patterns of Culture* (Boston: Houghton Mifflin Co., 1934), pp. 37-38.

The manner in which artistic activity is related to the living patterns which the group exhibits—its religious beliefs and practices, its economic arrangements, its family structure, to name a few—shows great variation from group to group. One of the most striking examples of this variation may be found in a comparison of the function of the arts in Soviet Russia with the role which they played in Medieval Europe. In the latter artistic expression resulted largely from religious motivation, whereas in the former it is dominated by a political and economic ideology and religion is not recognized as a valid area of experience.

In addition to the difference in patterning by which the arts are interwoven with other culture traits, we also find enormous differences in the artistic achievements of different cultures. Observance of this fact gives rise to several questions with respect to the relations between social forms and cultural achievement. Are there any characteristics which can be stated as essential to a society for high artistic achievement? What is the desirable relationship between the individual artist and the group? An attempt will be made to answer these questions with particular reference to the theory of art which was presented in Chapter IV.

RELATION BETWEEN SOCIAL FORMS AND
CULTURAL ACHIEVEMENT

In *Art as Experience*, John Dewey has shown that ". . . every culture has its own collective individuality." "Like the individuality of the person from whom the work of art issues," he says, "this collective individuality leaves its indelible imprint upon the art that is produced." [2] It seems that it may be possible to push this analogy one step further and say that just as the individual artist must attain personal integration as a condition for valid artistic expression, so a culture must be socially integrated if it is to be distinguished by its artistic achievements. Herbert Read has pointed to the art of Medieval Europe, as exemplified in the Gothic cathedral, to support this thesis. [3] In the

[2] From *Art as Experience*, p. 330, by John Dewey. Copyright, 1936, by John Dewey. Courtesy G. P. Putnam's Sons.
[3] Herbert Read, *The Grass Roots of Art* (New York: Wittenborn, Schultz, Inc., 1949), pp. 46 ff.

life of the Middle Ages, religious devotion was the source of a
unity strong enough to override all the frictions and divisions
which were also a part of that period. In a similar manner, the
period of great productivity in the Greek civilization was distinguished by its unity and integration. By contrast, Dewey
points to the decay of art in the Alexandrian period, which, he
says, "is a sign of the general loss of civic consciousness that accompanied the eclipse of city-states and the rise of a conglomerate imperialism." [4] These examples serve merely to illustrate
the fact that there is considerable historical evidence to support
this argument.

Indeed, if one accepts the theory presented in Chapter IV of
the relation of art to experience, it would be difficult to deny the
importance of social integration for artistic achievement. What
is said of the experience of an individual may also be said of the
experience of a culture that only as it is an integrated and dynamic unity will it encourage esthetic achievement. The individual artist is not born to his role but is a product of the culture
into which he is born and in which he lives. It is only in very
rare cases that a culture which is torn and divided will produce
individuals with the wholeness of vision and unity of purpose
from which rare artistic achievement springs. This is the genius
who, by virtue of his penetrating insights, is able to see beyond
the immediate disunity to larger, more comprehensive relationships. Such an individual, if and when he does occur, serves only
to emphasize the general cultural poverty of his milieu; and we
can only conjecture as to the number of potential talents that
have not flowered because the earth was sterile.

A second condition for cultural growth is a corollary of the
first one: that there must be a broad base of cultural achievement
and understanding within the group. A parallel may be drawn
here in the scientific advances which have been made in our own
culture. Our entire civilization is scientifically oriented; we tend
to think almost exclusively in scientific terms and to make all
our evaluations in terms of scientific fact. That, at least, is our
ideal of behavior however far we may fall short of it in actual
fact. Such a predisposition toward a scientific way of life is

[4] Dewey, *op. cit.*, p. 328.

surely one of the chief reasons for the tremendous scientific achievements which characterize our age and the emergence of so many first-rate minds in the fields of science. In a culture which was indifferent or hostile to the scientific attitude and to the fruits of science such a development would be unthinkable. In the same way, the arts can prosper only when they are accepted as a normal and natural part of the fabric of living. The potential artist who grows up in an environment indifferent or hostile to the arts is apt to deny his potentialities and turn to a field of endeavor which receives greater social approbation. If he perseveres regardless of social pressures, it is an act of defiance which forces him into isolation where he creates for himself and for other artists similarly isolated. Thus a wide gulf separates the artist from the public and a vicious circle is set in motion. As the artist is rejected he directs his work more exclusively to his fellow practitioners and tends to become esoteric, with the result that as he becomes less comprehensible to the layman the rejection which he suffers becomes more violent. The consequence is cultural disintegration which, as we have seen, is an enemy of artistic achievement.

Herbert Read, in *Art and Society*, maintains that this is the inevitable fate of the artist—that because of his finer perceptions, his utter preoccupation with the esthetic aspects of living, and his consequent divergences from a "normal" vision of the world, he is bound to be regarded as a misfit, often of comic proportions.[5] It is somewhat difficult to reconcile this point of view with other, more recent, statements by the same author. For example, in *The Grass Roots of Art*, he postulates as one of the necessary conditions for the development of great architecture a widespread interest and support on the part of the people.[6] In any case, the reason for citing the earlier statements here is not merely to criticize their author but rather to point out a widely held belief regarding the artist's relation to society. There seems to be as little justification for believing this is the inevitable fate of the artist as for believing that Albert Einstein must be re-

[5] Herbert Read, *Art and Society* (New York: Pantheon Books, 1950), pp. 71-72.
[6] Read, *The Grass Roots of Art*, pp. 47 ff.

garded as a misfit because his scientific perceptions are so far in advance of those of the average man. Einstein is regarded as a person who does better than anyone else something which is good in itself to do. This attitude seems also to disregard the position which artists have enjoyed in other cultures. Margaret Mead has described the position of the artist in primitive societies as follows:

. . . in primitive societies, the artist is not a separate person, having no immediate relationship to the economic processes and everyday experiences of his society. The concept of the artist whose gifts set him apart, or who only becomes an artist because his life history has set him apart, is almost wholly lacking. The artist, instead, is a person who does best something that other people, many other people, do less well. His products, whether he be choreographer or dancer, flutist or pot-maker, or carver of the temple gate, are seen as differing in degree but not in kind from the achievements of the less gifted among his fellow citizens. The concept of the artist as different in kind is fatal to the development of any adequate artistic form which will satisfy all of the sensibilities which are developed in individuals reared under the impact of these forms.[7]

Another condition which has been specified by Read, with respect to architecture, as necessary for outstanding achievement, is smallness of the group. He argues that in the history of architecture increase in size has always been accompanied by a decline in cultural vitality.[8] Dewey, in the passage quoted above (page 96) indicates that the increased size of the Alexandrian state was related to the decline of the arts. He speaks, however, of a "conglomerate imperialism" which transfers the emphasis from the mere fact of size to the fact of social disintegration. It seems a reasonable supposition that the basic factor is not size alone but the relative unwieldiness, and consequently the poorer integration, which has generally characterized very large culture groups. Whether or not this is an inevitable accompaniment of large and highly complex societies cannot be determined here. If it is, this does surely not bode well for the future of the arts nor of civilization itself, for the tendency is

[7] Margaret Mead, "Art and Reality," *College Art Journal*, II (May 1943), 120.
[8] Read, *The Grass Roots of Art*, pp. 30–31.

overwhelmingly in the direction of larger societal organizations. In the face of this trend we can only turn our attention to the means whereby a higher level of integration may be achieved since it is neither possible nor desirable to turn time back.

As we have seen in Chapter IV, the validity of artistic expression depends largely upon the artist's integrity and the extent to which he is able to give artistic form to his own highly personal feelings and emotions. This implies a social organization which not only protects, but also values and respects the individual's integrity, and encourages freedom of thought and movement. It may be seen that this is merely a specific application of a basic principle of democratic living, and what has been said in Part One regarding the relation of the individual to the group provides a background for discussing the freedom of the artist in society. We saw there that successful democratic living depends upon the full release and development of the individual's creative powers and that only in this way can the group realize its full strength and vitality. Because of its highly personal nature, it is especially true of artistic expression that it cannot be forced through edict and coercion. It must be allowed to grow naturally and normally in an environment of freedom.

It is necessary, however, to distinguish between freedom and irresponsibility. Mention has been made earlier of the concept of the arts as a retreat from living, a means of escape from the sordid facts of existence into a world of fantasy. There can be no doubt that this has provided the motivation for some artistic achievements of very high quality. The works of such men as Odilon Redon and Morris Graves are cases in point. Other artists, such as James Baron Ensor, have been moved to expression largely by feelings of antagonism and bitterness toward the society in which they lived. The achievements of such artists cannot be denied. However, the question to be asked is whether a society which stimulates its artists to production by antagonizing them or driving them into seclusion is realizing its full creative potentialities. The idea is frequently stated that creative genius necessarily involves a degree of isolation from society and an antagonism to socially accepted standards. There may, however, be a difference between antagonism to socially accepted standards and an antagonism to society. If the artist is to be more than an inert reflection of the group in which he lives, he must necessarily be devoted to reshaping and refining the values of living. But this can occur most successfully in a climate of mutual interest and respect between the artist and his society. Horney[9] is among a growing group of psychoanalysts who support the view that individuals achieve what they do achieve in spite of, rather than because of, their emotional conflicts. We may ask, therefore, with respect to the particular cases cited above, how much greater their contributions might have been had they achieved a fuller measure of integration with their societies.

There are, of course, two faces to the problem. On the one hand is the kind of artist whose inner compulsions lead to self-isolation and social irresponsibility. On the other hand is the kind of society whose attitudes toward matters of esthetic interest are such as to shut the artist off from the group, to ostracize him. These two processes do not occur separately; each acts upon and intensifies the other, and the gulf of separation widens. To reach a happier state of understanding, therefore, is a problem for both the artist and the layman, because it is a problem of achieving a fuller integration and a condition of mutually beneficial interaction.

ART AND THE EXPRESSION OF GROUP VALUES

It is a truism that art is a mirror of society. Anthropologists and historians have long recognized the value of the arts as resources for studying the beliefs and ideals, the manners and patterns of living of the society in which they were produced. It seems inevitable that this should be true, for the artist, like any human being, is shaped by the culture in which he lives. It is inconceivable that Pericles should have expressed himself in the manner of a Medieval sculptor, or that the music of a twentieth-century composer could take the same form as the compositions of a Palestrina or a Brahms. The Pre-Raphaelites provide a notable example of artists who attempted to recapture the faith and

[9] Karen Horney, *Our Inner Conflicts: A Constructive Theory of Neurosis* (New York: W. W. Norton and Co., 1945), 250 pp.

the behavior of an earlier age. The art which they produced offers the only evidence necessary of their indifferent success in trying to express the ideals of an age not their own.

At the same time, it would be a mistake to assert that the arts are always a direct expression of the dominant motivations of a culture. In the case of the Pre-Raphaelites, their attempt to return to the ways of the Medieval artists was a violent protest against the crudities and barbarities of a rising industrial system in which they saw nothing but evil. But the mere fact of their revolt gives us insights into the culture of nineteenth-century England.

Mumford, in the following passage, describes the tremendous impact of the industrial city on Van Gogh:

Van Gogh knew the paleotechnic city in its most complete gloom, the foul, bedraggled, gas-lighted London of the seventies: he also knew the very source of its dark energies, places like the mines at La Borinage where he had lived with the miners. In his early pictures he absorbed and courageously faced the most sinister parts of his environment: he painted the gnarled bodies of the miners, the almost animal stupor of their faces, bent over the bare dinner of potatoes, the eternal blacks, grays, dark blues, and soiled yellows of their poverty-stricken homes.[10]

In another passage, Mumford draws striking parallels between the modern symphonic form and the industrial society in which it developed:

. . . music, in the creation of the new orchestra, and in the scope and power and movement of the new symphonies, became in a singularly representative way, the ideal counterpart of industrial society.

. . . . .

All the instruments were now scientifically calibrated: the production of sound became, within limits, standardized and predictable. And with the increase in the number of instruments, the division of labor within the orchestra corresponded to that of the factory: the division of the process itself became noticeable in the newer symphonies. The leader was the superintendent and production manager, in charge of the manufacture and assembly of the product,

[10] Lewis Mumford, *Technics and Civilization* (New York: Harcourt, Brace and Co., 1934), pp. 200–01.

namely the piece of music, while the composer corresponded to the inventor, engineer, and designer, who had to calculate on paper, with the aid of such minor instruments as the piano, the nature of the ultimate product—working out its last detail before a single step was made in the factory.[11]

In *The Way Beyond "Art,"* [12] Dorner has shown how, throughout the history of the visual arts, the concept of space and the manner of representing it have closely paralleled the ideas which men had of time and space and of their own relation to the world and to the cosmos. These examples are sufficient to indicate that there are countless ways in which the artists of a period or a culture are influenced, both directly and indirectly, by the environment in which they work, and thus reflect the environment itself. In further support of this concept, it would be possible to mention the developments in architecture which have accompanied new materials and methods for building, the influence on the Impressionist painters of the scientific research of Chevreul, and the extensive influence of psychoanalytic theory on the work of the Surrealists. Further discussion of this point scarcely seems necessary. The question which may be asked, however, is whether this presents the total picture of the social role of the arts. Are they always and only a passive agent mirroring the deeper currents of a culture, or do they play a more active role?

There would seem to be ample evidence that the arts do play an active part in shaping men's thoughts and behavior. That they can be powerful instruments of propaganda we know well enough from observation of the way they function in present-day totalitarian societies. It should be noted here that an evaluation of art in terms of its propaganda value is not an esthetic evaluation any more than is the evaluation of a building in terms of its conformance to standards of sanitation. The fact must be recognized, however, that the arts may be powerful instruments for propaganda and have frequently been used as such. In fact, as Northrop has pointed out, a large proportion of Western art

[11] *Ibid.,* p. 202.
[12] Alexander Dorner, *The Way Beyond "Art."* (New York: Wittenborn, Schultz, Inc., 1947), 244 pp.

has been, to a greater or lesser degree, in the service of ideology.[13]

There are other ways in which the arts, as arts, operate as active social forces. Dewey, in speaking of the art of the Church, says the following:

The historian of intellectual life will emphasize the dogmas of the Church; the historian of political institutions, the development of law and authority by means of the ecclesiastical institution. But the influence that counted in the daily lives of the mass of the people and that gave them a sense of unity was constituted, it is safe to surmise, by sacraments, by song and pictures, by rite and ceremony, all having an esthetic strand, more than by any other one thing.[14]

This is an example where the esthetic experience itself—the towering beauty of the cathedral, the inspiring form of the Mass, the richness and splendor of the vestments, the pure beauty of the music—exerted a powerful influence for social unity and for the continuity of established values.

Goldwater, in *Modern Art in Your Life*, has shown the extent to which the vision of the artist has played a part in shaping our everyday environment. He says:

As the artist's concepts are molded by the trends and aspirations of his age, so in turn he molds the appearance of objects around him. The role of a machine civilization in fathering Mondrian's love of the right angle and the clean, flat surface may be argued, but there is no doubt that his work gives form to the passionate concern with mathematical order that made mechanization possible and that *the esthetic of his pictures has entered into our way of seeing the world.*

When the architect strips his walls of ornament, when the jacket designer makes up his page with a few rigorous lines against large immaculate areas, when the package designer limits his appeal to square-cut letters and a minimum of balanced rectangles, they all share Mondrian's delight in a bold and subtle simplicity. In like fashion, the advertising artist, silhouetting his product against a dramatic deep and empty space, accepts the surrealist vision, while the furniture designer bends his plywood into freely molded shapes that have their counterpart in the works of Arp and Miro.[15]

[13] F. S. C. Northrop, *The Meeting of East and West* (New York: The Macmillan Company, 1946), pp. 360 ff.
[14] Dewey, *op. cit.*, p. 329.
[15] Robert Goldwater, *Modern Art in Your Life* (New York: Museum of Modern Art, 1949), p. 5. Italics the present author's.

Here is a case where the "fine" artist—the painter or the sculptor—has, through the influence of his fresh vision, been instrumental in shaping the world in which we live, giving new form to the objects of everyday living, and thereby introducing new patterns of behavior into the culture. The force of the arts in renewing and altering our vision and our values has been emphasized by Edman when he shows that the strongest opposition to them comes from the Puritan, the Statesman, and the Practical Man. The Puritan fears the power of the arts to awaken the sensuous life and thus divert the individual from the pursuit of the higher spiritual life. "The Statesman has always been aware how the artist, through an imaginative touching of the passions of a nation, may destroy the long-standing pillars of habit, the ancient discipline of institutions or of reason." And the Practical Man sees in the arts a futile diversion from the business of "real life." [16] Each, for his own reason, fears the arts for their power to change the ways of men.

There is another aspect of the arts which is taking on increasing importance in a world whose physical dimensions are constantly shrinking. Because they speak so eloquently of the ways of living and believing in the culture from which they spring, they can be a powerful device for the furthering of intercultural understanding. Sociologists and political scientists can give us much valuable information about the patterns of contemporary Japanese culture; but to see a modern Japanese motion picture or hear modern Japanese music is to gain new insights into the powerful influences of Western culture and the way in which they have been adapted to traditional forms of Japanese living. To hear the music and see the dancing of the Haitian people is to experience directly an important aspect of their culture, and to understand better the rhythms of their living. The paintings of the German Expressionists reveal accurately the currents of feeling which were stirring in Germany in the earlier part of this century. Clearly, the arts of a foreign people may seem strange and discordant to eyes and ears that are untutored or that do not open readily to new experiences. To the mind that is closed the

[16] Irwin Edman, *Arts and the Man* (New York: W. W. Norton and Co., 1939), pp. 47 ff.

music of the Chinese will be only another example of the strange-
ness, the peculiarity, and perhaps the inferiority, of the Chinese
people. There are many languages in the arts just as there are
many spoken languages, and they can be learned only by the
person who is receptive and eager for the new experiences that
they can give him. As Edman has said:

[The arts] are utterances of the quality of experience itself, and that
quality is at once more immediate and more absolute than the language of apparently sober and responsible practical prose discourse.
The syntax of the arts, if it is not the syntax of nature, is at least a
more adequate grammar for saying what men feel and see and hear
than any of the more generalized periphrasis of analytical diction.
The truth *of* things rather than the truth *about* them finds its articu-
lateness in the varied languages of the arts.[17]

It is precisely because the artist deals with the truth *of* things
rather than the truth *about* things—because he presents to us the
realities of living apprehended with emotion and feeling—that
he can give us actual knowledge of the world in which we live
and a vision of the world in which we might live. We have
fallen into the error of assuming that the means and materials
which science provides can give us our direction, can build the
future for us. But, as MacMurray has pointed out, "That capacity depends upon the knowledge of actual reality: not the information about it that science gives, but the grasp of it that the
artist possesses." [18] By revealing to us the deeper meanings of
reality, by giving us actual knowledge of the world and of ourselves, the artist can, if we are attentive to him, lead us to new
ways of feeling and believing—toward the realization of a better
and fuller life.

[17] *Ibid.*, p. 142.
[18] John MacMurray, *Reason and Emotion*, p. 167. Copyright, 1938, D. Appleton-Century Company, Inc.

Chapter VI

CONTEMPORARY LIVING AND THE ARTS

The two preceding chapters have dealt, in a general way, with the role of the arts in the life of the individual and in the life of the culture. Such a generalized discussion is a necessary preliminary to the consideration of any specific situation. But generalization can be profitably applied to particular cases only when the conditions of the particular case are known. In order, therefore, to gain an adequate picture of the role of the arts—both actual and potential—in contemporary American culture, it is necessary to look more closely at some of the patterns which characterize life in America today. With this as a background, it should then be possible to indicate, in more precise terms, how the arts can make the fullest possible contribution to the enrichment of American life.

DOMINANT TRENDS IN THE AMERICAN CULTURE

THE SCIENTIFIC BIAS

Reference has already been made to the extreme preoccupation of the Western world with the scientific aspects of reality.

The roots and causes of this bias in favor of the scientific approach to living go far back into the history of the culture and are beyond the scope of the present discussion. It is necessary here only to recognize the fact of its existence.

The word "bias" has been used advisedly here, for our attitude toward science has been, not that it is *a* means for achieving the good life, but that it is *the only* means for achieving it. The fact that we have resisted the inroads of science into some aspects of our living does not constitute a valid contradiction of this statement. It is certainly true that there is evidence on every hand of our refusal to accept scientific facts which threaten to demolish prejudices. But though we may waver momentarily in our allegiance to science, we do not recognize any other method of knowledge as having equal validity. What we know scientifically is fact and all else is merely opinion. We can believe only what has been verified in the scientist's laboratory.

The "halo effect" of our faith in science has been such as to destroy our faith in any other method of knowledge. This is perhaps most widely recognized in the conflict between science and religion. As the frontiers of science have advanced, many religious dogmas have been revealed as having no basis in scientific fact. What we have failed to recognize is that dogmas are only the outward signs of a religious faith, and instead of merely rejecting the dogmas we have rejected the religious experience itself. This rejection has occurred not only because specific dogmas have been discredited, but also because the religious experience itself is not subject to scientific verification.

Precisely the same thing has happened in the area of esthetic experience. The conflict has not been as easily observable because, in the first place, esthetic interests have not been as well organized as religious interests. In the second place, esthetic activity has never been as closely tied to specific dogmas which might be revealed as scientifically false. However, esthetic experience has been equally discredited with religious experience. It is regarded, not as a complementary way to knowledge, but as a kind of experience which is basically anti-scientific and therefore to be avoided by rational and intelligent people.

Science has become our sacred cow, our only means to salvation. Our faith has been such that we have believed science capable, not only of helping us move toward our goals, but also of revealing to us what our goals should be. It has, in fact, become a goal in itself, for it alone can guide us to knowledge and to truth.

THE MATERIALISTIC APPROACH TO LIVING

A striking characteristic of our culture is the tendency to identify progress and the realization of the good life almost exclusively with the improvement and multiplication of the material accompaniments of living. As Mumford has said, ". . . there is supposed to be a close relationship between well-being and the number of bath-tubs, motor cars, and similar machine-made products that one may possess." [1] He points out, furthermore, that because of our capitalist economy, our aim is not merely to satisfy the needs of life, but rather, ". . . to expand toward an indefinite limit the amount of physical equipment that is applied to living. . . ." This he has called "purposeless materialism." "Its particular defect," he says, "is that it casts a shadow of reproach upon all the non-material interests and occupations of mankind; in particular, it condemns liberal and esthetic interests because 'they serve no useful purpose.' " [2]

At the same time that we regard the production of goods as our ultimate ideal, we evaluate personal success in terms of financial success. The man who has "made good" is the man who has amassed the greatest fortune and can thereby accumulate the greatest quantity of material goods. It is only the rare individual who will refuse a high-paying job because it offers less promise of personal satisfaction than another job which is financially less rewarding. It is true that such people do command a certain kind of respect, but it is the kind of respect usually reserved for martyrs who have made great sacrifices to uphold their principles. They are recognized as being distinctly different from the usual run of people, and it is generally considered fortunate for the welfare of the country that there are but few of them. Their

---

[1] Lewis Mumford, *Technics and Civilization* (New York: Harcourt, Brace and Co., 1934), p. 273.
[2] *Loc. cit.*

attitude smacks almost of selfishness because they refuse to sacrifice their own happiness for the realization of our national ideal of commercial progress.

As Mumford has suggested, our evaluations tend to be exclusively in terms of practical usefulness. The things of greatest value are those which promise to increase our income, and thus make it possible to acquire more goods, or to increase our physical well-being. Where land values are high we create no parks, because parks don't yield profits and office buildings do; the most worth-while college courses are those which will increase our earning power; the best foods are those which are the easiest to prepare or which have been prepared for us.

It would obviously be false to say that we are motivated entirely by materialistic values. There are, in fact, encouraging signs that these values, although still enjoying a position of supremacy, may not have the same relative importance in the minds of many people that they once had. For evidence we may look at the increasing interest which is being shown in participation in the arts; the growing attendance at concerts, at the theater, and at art exhibitions; the increase in church membership; and, no less important, the changing emphasis in education away from narrowly conceived vocational objectives to a more comprehensive view of the role of education as the development of the total personality.

In a sense, however, these countercurrents only serve to emphasize, by virtue of the fact that they *are* countercurrents, the very important place which materialistic values have in our living. Without belittling their importance or denying that they represent a trend of considerable proportion, it may still be said that, by and large, our dominant motives have to do with the material goods of living, and before these all others must yield.

THE INDUSTRIAL TECHNOLOGY

Out of the interactions of these two factors—our devotion to science and our predominantly materialistic values—has developed the industrial technology which is probably one of the greatest, and also one of the most characteristic, of our achievements. This statement is by no means meant to confuse technology with science. Indeed, Mumford has shown that the early inventions which gave rise to technology occurred, by and large, without the direct aid of science.[3] However, as the scientific method has gained a firmer foothold, it has provided increasingly the initiative for invention and technological development. In the efficiency expert, we find the methods of science applied to the technological process itself.

Basically, the process of technology is the application of scientific methods to the problems of production. It involves the detailed analysis of skills and of procedures and the breaking down of the total process of production into a number of separate and discrete operations. Like the machines which they operate, the individuals involved in production are the object of careful analysis and themselves become mechanisms for the completion of separate parts of the productive process.

It is only by this method of analysis and specialization that the enormous complexity of our industrial system has been possible. When each individual involved in the production of a complex mechanism, such as a motor car, needs to perform only one simple operation, he can learn his task quickly, perform it efficiently, and be easily replaced. Thus, through the specialization of talents and of operations, our productive capacity has been increased many times over.

Technology has become such an important part of the fabric of our living that it is scarcely possible to think of any area of activity which it has not touched in one way or another. Because of its very obvious advantages in the production of goods, we have tended to accept it unquestioningly and to apply it wherever it gives promise of greater efficiency—efficiency being defined almost exclusively in terms of quantity and speed of production. Libraries, schools, hospitals, theaters, social agencies, department stores—all are organized for quantity production in terms of highly specialized functions.

The tremendous benefits which we have realized as a result of our technological ingenuity have led us to accept it just as we have accepted science and a materialistic scale of values—without question or reservation. That the benefits have been tre-

[3] *Ibid.*, p. 215.

mendous there can be no doubt; for evidence we have only to look at our high standard of living. However, it is necessary to ask ourselves whether our intense devotion to scientific and materialistic goals and the rigorous application of the technological method to all the areas of our living have been as completely productive of a better life as we have generally assumed them to be. What are some of the effects of these major trends upon the patterns of our daily living?

SOME EFFECTS OF DOMINANT CULTURAL TRENDS

INCREASED PRODUCTION OF GOODS AND
HIGHER STANDARD OF LIVING

This aspect of our culture is so obvious as scarcely to need mention. The United States is capable of producing more goods in a shorter time than any other nation. As a result, our general standard of living is the highest that has been attained in the history of the human race, if it is measured purely in terms of material comforts and benefits. We have more food, more clothing, better houses, more motorcars and refrigerators, more television sets and motion picture theaters than any other country in the world. Each day we are greeted with new products in a market already overflowing with a variety of goods.

There is, of course, an enormous differential in the amount of goods which individuals are able to acquire because of the wide range in economic status (see p. 24). However, through minimum wage laws, social security benefits, increased taxation of high incomes, and the activities of organized labor, efforts are constantly being made to counteract the tendencies toward a greater concentration of wealth. In fact the vitality of our capitalist economy is dependent upon the existence of a large buying public. Whatever the particular facts about the distribution of wealth may be, for those who can afford them the material comforts of living are more easily available here than elsewhere, and our goal is to make them more easily available to a constantly larger proportion of the population. America is indeed the land of plenty.

INCREASE IN LEISURE TIME

The productive capacity of the machine has been such that the length of the average working day has been greatly shortened as compared with that of pre-industrial days or the early days of industrial development. This is a trend which we can expect to continue, for more powerful and more productive machines are being constantly produced, and the necessity for long hours of manual labor is correspondingly eliminated. The potentialities of atomic energy for increasing productive capacity and thereby lightening the individual's work load can at present only be guessed.

In addition to the development of more powerful and productive machines, scientific studies of the worker's reactions and movements have been an important factor in increasing his effectiveness of operation, enabling him to do more work in less time. Time and motion studies, the analysis of special skills and the development of tests to measure them, the study of morale factors in employment situations—these have been some of the most fruitful approaches for increasing the efficiency of the worker. It is true that these measures have rarely, if ever, been undertaken for the express purpose of lightening the individual's work load and giving him a shorter working day, but this has been, over a long period of time, the net result.

There has not been a one-to-one correspondence between the reduction in working hours and the increase in leisure time. The much greater complexity of contemporary living patterns has tended, to some extent, to vitiate the gains which have been made. For example, although the worker in the pre-industrial era may have spent twelve or fourteen hours a day at his work, in most cases he lived where he worked; by comparison, although the modern factory or office employee may spend only half as much time in terms of working hours, it is not uncommon for him to spend two or more hours each day getting from his home to his work and back again. He must keep his car in repair, fill out income tax returns, get his children to and from school, and take care of all the many details of living which are part of an extremely complex social organization. But in the over-all picture, the American worker spends the minimum number of hours in productive labor and has the maximum amount of leisure time in which to enjoy the fruits of his labors.

INTERDEPENDENCE AND ISOLATION

One of the most significant aspects of our mechanical society is the extent to which interdependence is a necessary condition for survival. In commenting on this aspect of the culture, Mumford has said:

Individual self-sufficiency is another way of saying technological crudeness: as our technics becomes more refined it becomes impossible to work the machine without large-scale collective cooperation, and in the long run a high technics is possible only on a basis of world-wide trade and intellectual intercourse. The machine has broken down the relative isolation—never complete in the most primitive societies—of the handicraft period: it has intensified the need for collective effort and collective order.[4]

Because of the greater interdependence which has come with technological development, the effective environment of the individual has been increased many times over. In a primitive society the individual was rarely affected by anything that occurred beyond the limits of his own small community or the few communities with which his own group had intercourse. The orbit of his life was circumscribed by the physical distance he could travel on foot or in crude conveyances. Today an individual living in the middle of Missouri feels the impact of events in the Far East nearly as quickly as he is influenced by occurrences in his own community. The range and extent of environmental influences has been immeasurably increased as technology has eliminated the safe isolation of local and national boundaries.

While technology has brought with it a greater interdependence between individuals and between groups, it has also brought a depersonalization of relationships. Our contacts with people tend frequently to be regarded more as means to ends which we cannot achieve by ourselves than as ends which are worth while in themselves. Also, because of the extreme specialization which characterizes the culture, contacts, while more varied, are at the

[4] *Ibid.*, p. 280.

same time more superficial because they are unidimensional. The grocer is the man from whom we get food; the filling station attendant is a source of motor fuel; the labor union is the organization which is joined to secure better working conditions; business associates are that and nothing more. Each of the various associations of modern life tends to be made on the basis of a single need or a single area of activity. The increase in number and variety of contacts, therefore, is accompanied by a decrease in depth and richness of meaning.

Reference has already been made to the increased size of our social institutions as a factor contributing to the individual's feeling of remoteness and isolation (see pp. 37–38). Our vast organizations of business and of government, of education and of recreation, have, in many cases, lost their human scale. As far as the individual is concerned, his feeling is not one of *interdependence*, but merely of *dependence*. He is well aware of his dependence on the complex institutions and organizations which pattern his living, but he has little feeling of identification with them or responsibility for them because they seem, by virtue of their size and remoteness, to be entities in themselves which move and operate quite independently of individual people.

The feeling of dependency without a corresponding sense of responsibility is extremely damaging to the individual's own sense of worth and integrity. Because of his feeling of helplessness and dependence he becomes, at the least, apathetic and, at the worst, antagonistic, and he identifies himself less, rather than more, with the groups and organizations which impinge upon his life. They are regarded as instrumentalities for the achievement of desired ends. He feels no personal responsibility but only the desire to get as much as he can out of each contact he makes.

The tendency toward isolation and lack of integration and understanding between groups was discussed at some length in Part One. It is only necessary to mention it here as another aspect of this problem, as a countercurrent to the increased interdependence which technology has brought with it. Interdependence does not necessarily mean mutuality of interest or cooperative behavior. The relationship between labor and capital is a case in point. Their interdependence is obvious. Neither could survive without the other. Yet at the same time, the depth of their antagonism is probably without parallel in the American culture. It is, in fact, because they are so dependent on each other that the conflict exists. If each were completely self-sufficient, there would be no occasion for strife or disagreement.

Such differences, arising as they do out of conflicting purposes with respect to a common enterprise, are to be distinguished from the isolation which frequently results from extremely narrow specialization. The whole-hearted pursuit of a special interest may so effectively demarcate a group from its environment that intergroup contacts are held to a minimum and those contacts which are maintained have only a tangential relation to the central interest of the group. Possibly the most extreme example of such isolation may be found in certain religious orders who, in the pursuit of holiness, consciously strive to cut the ties binding them to the outside world. They never achieve complete independence because they must look to other groups and other people for many of the physical goods of living. But with respect to the particular interest which motivates their isolation, there is a minimum of interchange and their central movement is inward rather than outward. Their primary interest moves them away from other groups, and interdependence is held at the "subsistence" level. The same phenomenon may be observed in any group pursuing a special interest; the degree of isolation depends largely upon the extent to which the special interest becomes an all-absorbing end disjoined from the larger context of the culture.

LOSS OF OPPORTUNITY FOR CREATIVE ACTIVITY IN DAILY PURSUITS

We have seen how technological efficiency depends, to a very great degree, upon two factors: fragmentation of productive processes and automatization of operation. In *Mechanization Takes Command*, Giedion has given an example of the lengths to which we have gone in specializing and routinizing the individual's activities in productive employment:

In a Chicago packing house, hogs, hanging head downwards, moved uninterruptedly past a staunch Negro woman at the curve of the conveyor system. Her task was to stamp with a rubber stamp, the carcasses examined by the inspector. With a sweeping movement, she smacked the rubber stamp on each skin.

Perhaps we start from false premises; but in an outside observer a strange feeling was aroused: a creature of the human race trained to do nothing else but, day after day, eight hours a day, stamp thousand after thousand of carcasses in four places.[5]

This example could be paralleled in any large factory or business concern. The pushing of a lever, the tightening of a bolt, the pressing of typewriter keys, the counting and sorting of articles—these are typical work activities in an efficient factory or office. Successful operation depends, to a large extent, upon the elimination of the human factor, the complete mechanization of the worker himself.

The need for human skill and craftsmanship is thus reduced to a minimum. It is true that there are many jobs which require a high order of dexterity, but it is generally dexterity in performing a simple repetitive operation with machine-like regularity. Craftsmanship—the working and shaping of materials— and the knowledge of materials which must accompany it, are scarcely necessary for successful job performance.

It is not only in the factory and the office that the need for skill has been eliminated. It is equally true in many other areas of living. Skills in cooking and sewing, for example, are becoming less and less common among American women because clothes are ready-made and so too is food to an increasing degree. The motorcar has been perfected to the point where it requires the very minimum of intelligence or skill for its operation. To be entertained by music, an individual no longer needs to develop his musical skills; he need only be able to twirl a few knobs on the face of a cabinet. In many ways mechanization has decreased both the need and the opportunity for the development of human skills.

The depersonalization of machine production has been pointed out by Eric Gill:

[5] Siegfried Giedion, *Mechanization Takes Command* (New York: Oxford University Press, 1948), p. 124.

If I take a piece of iron and with my fingers and various tools . . . shape that iron into the shape of a box, *because that is the kind of man I am*—that is one thing. If I take a similar piece of iron and put it into one end of a machine and it comes out at the other end a box, *because that's the kind of . . . machine it is*—that is quite another thing.[6]

The depersonalization is due here to the intervention of the machine between the worker and the product. It is the machine which now controls the product rather than the person. The same kind of depersonalization occurs also wherever activities become extremely specialized and routinized, whether we are dealing with machine processes or hand processes. The woman described by Giedion was herself behaving like a machine—the human factor, insofar as possible, had been eliminated from her work. In the same way, the filing clerk, whose job in an office is to file one kind of correspondence, let us say, for one particular department, increases her efficiency as she is able to operate less like a human being and more like a machine.

In all these examples, the common characteristic to be found is the separation of means from ends. In the pre-industrial era, the craftsman was a maker of things—harnesses, houses, lamps, candles, shoes, or sabers. He controlled the entire process of manufacture from beginning to end and each operation in the total process he was able to see in its relation to the end goal. As work becomes more routinized and specialized the relationship between means and ends becomes partially or totally obscured. The modern worker is not a maker—but a mere doer —of things; he is an operator of a machine, and whether the machine turns out perfume bottles or pencil sharpeners makes little difference. He has no emotional connection with the product of his labors. Gorer has commented on this aspect of American life as follows:

It is worth nothing that the extremely slight emotional connection with one's job and, often, ignorance of the end-product are not consciously felt by Americans to be a deprivation. When the details of the manufacture of the atomic bomb were made public, most Europeans (I among them) and a few Americans with European values

[6] Eric Gill, *Art* (London: John Lane, 1934), p. 115.

thought that the tens of thousands of workers engaged in work whose end-product nobody knew must have felt supremely demoralized, dispirited, and frustrated, almost as though they were engaged in forced prison labor. But this was not the case. Numerous conversations with former workers at Oak Ridge and other atomic plants demonstrated that it was not felt to be different (except for the isolation) from any other job paying similar money for similar hours.[7]

We may seriously question the distinction which Gorer implies between the attitudes of the American worker and the European worker. It seems much more likely that the attitude described here results from the characteristic conditions which are a part of any large-scale industrial operation. The product which results from the individual's labor no longer has any immediate significance for him, and in its place is the monetary reward which he receives for his services. He cannot relate himself to the product because he has no connection with it beyond the one simple operation which he completes and which defines the limits of his responsibility. In any job which has become highly specialized, whether it is concerned with producing goods or with providing services, there is the tendency for the individual to become merely a cog in a large wheel, having little or no idea of the purpose of the wheel of which he is a part, nor the manner in which it meshes with other wheels. This is not his concern; his only concern is to be an efficient cog.

Another important characteristic of technology is the premium set on standardization and uniformity. Mumford has shown how this is an essential characteristic of machine production:

Whereas handicraft, by the very nature of human work, exhibits constant variations and adaptations, and boasts of the fact that no two products are alike, machine work has just the opposite characteristic: it prides itself on the fact that the millionth motor car built to a specific pattern is exactly like the first. Speaking generally, the machine has replaced an unlimited series of variables with a limited number of constants: if the range of possibility is lessened, the area of prediction and control is increased.[8]

[7] Geoffrey Gorer, *The American People* (New York: W. W. Norton and Co., 1948), pp. 141–42.
[8] Mumford, *op. cit.*, pp. 277–78.

Mumford, in continuing his discussion, holds that the dangers of standardized products have been frequently overrated and that a certain amount of uniformity is essential for well-ordered living. He points out that standardization and repetition, "by pushing below the level of consciousness certain recurrent elements in our experience . . . free attention for the non-mechanical, the unexpected, the personal." [9] While this can scarcely be contradicted, it would be unwise to gloss over the possible effects of too great an emphasis on standardization, for it is equally true that when a high premium is placed on standardization itself, uniformity of behavior becomes the accepted mode and variations from the standard are viewed with disfavor; thus, rather than freeing attention for the "non-mechanical, the unexpected, the personal," it puts a checkrein on it.

In *Escape from Freedom*, Fromm has shown how conformity to a standard of behavior and automatization of response is one of the mechanisms whereby individuals attempt to escape the sense of isolation and aloneness which accompanies what he calls "negative freedom"—freedom *from* restraint—without a corresponding freedom *to* relate oneself spontaneously to the world:

To put it briefly, the individual ceases to be himself; he adopts entirely the kind of personality offered him by the cultural patterns; and he therefore becomes exactly as all others are and as they expect him to be. The discrepancy between "I" and the world disappears and with it the conscious fear of aloneness and powerlessness. This mechanism can be compared with the protective coloring some animals assume. They look so similar to their surroundings that they are hardly distinguishable from them. The person who gives up his individual self and becomes an automaton, identical with millions of other automatons around him, need not feel alone and anxious any more. But the price he pays, however, is high; it is the loss of his self.[10]

The essence of creative action is individuality of response— the solution of a problem in terms of the individual's assessment according to his particular values and his ways of working. It is the polar opposite of standardization and uniformity. While

[9] *Ibid.*, p. 278.
[10] Erich Fromm, *Escape from Freedom* (New York: Rinehart and Co., 1941), pp. 185–86.

standardization of the routine aspects of living may, as Mumford suggests, release our potentialities for creative activities of a more personal nature, putting a premium on uniformity routinizes and devitalizes those aspects of our living which should have the warmth of personality and individuality. The dilemma in which we find ourselves has two aspects. On the one hand, the material facts of our culture are such as to have seriously curtailed the opportunities for free, creative expression in the daily pursuits of living; on the other hand, in our attempts to escape from the isolation of a depersonalized culture, we have tended to repudiate our right and our need for individualized, creative living.

REJECTION OF ESTHETIC VALUES: SEPARATION
OF THE ARTS FROM LIVING

We have already seen how an emphasis on the scientific aspects of reality and a preoccupation with material values have, to a large extent, discredited the esthetic factor at least so far as the normal pursuits of living are concerned. As Haggerty has pointed out, "To men absorbed in the work of the world artists appear to be a cult and their work and conversation seem esoteric and almost mystical." [11] This statement carries several implications which deserve further attention.

In the first place, esthetic values are regarded as having no proper place in the affairs of daily living. As Dewey has said, ". . . many a person would be repelled rather than pleased if told that he enjoyed his casual recreations, in part at least, because of their esthetic quality." [12] Even more repellent is the idea that esthetic considerations are a proper part of the serious business of making a living. In all too many cases, it is true, the opportunities for esthetic experience in the individual's gainful employment have been reduced to a minimum if not altogether eliminated, but this very fact is an indication of the attitude that esthetic interests are of negligible importance in our daily pursuits. Furthermore, the individual whose work has been simplified and routinized to the endless repetition of a single operation,

[11] Melvin Haggerty, *Art a Way of Life* (Minneapolis: University of Minnesota Press, 1935), pp. 6–7.
[12] From *Art as Experience*, p. 5, by John Dewey. Copyright, 1936, by John Dewey. Courtesy G. P. Putnam's Sons.

while he may recognize that his work is dull and monotonous, would be appalled at the idea that it is so largely because it has been robbed of all esthetic value.

It may be argued that whether or not he recognizes this missing element in his activities as being the esthetic element is unimportant, it is enough that he is aware of the lack and the name he gives to it is of no consequence. This is undoubtedly true; it has, in fact, been said that folk art exists only so long as the people who produce it do not realize that it is art. It should be mentioned in passing that however true this may be ours is not a folk culture and the criteria which are applied to folk art cannot necessarily be applied to ours with equal validity. However, the central point, so far as this discussion is concerned, is the fact that in many cases the individual will willingly forego the esthetic quality in his daily work (by whatever name he may call it) merely for the sake of greater material gain. His job is evaluated in terms of how much he realizes from it in dollars and cents and all other considerations are, if not irrelevant, at least secondary.

A notable exception to this rejection of the esthetic factor may be found in the fields of industrial design and commercial design. The industrial designer, as the artist of the machine age, as well as the commercial artist, is achieving considerable stature in the world of business. However, his work, by and large, subserves materialistic ends. His prestige is measured not so much in terms of how good an artist he is but in terms of how effectively he can increase sales. It would be most unrealistic to deny or overlook the contributions which have been made to the enrichment of our environment by these means. But it does seem necessary to point out that our whole economy is so geared that final judgments in these matters are made in terms of economic returns and the value scale by which such judgments are made frequently bears little, if any, relationship to an esthetic scale of values.

This repudiation of esthetic values may be seen in other spheres of activity besides those which are primarily concerned with the business of making a living. Academic emphasis on intellectual accomplishment and on the scientific criteria of reality has resulted in an almost complete neglect of the emotional and intuitive factors in human behavior. Only recently have colleges begun to recognize work in the arts as having sufficient academic "respectability" to give them a place in the program of instruction. And in many instances where they have been admitted, they have been so intellectualized as to reduce seriously the contributions which they might make to the enrichment of living.

Even in an area such as the theater, which is generally recognized to be an art form, there is a clear distinction between the "art" theater and the commercial theater, and any Broadway producer is wary of a production which has an aura of art about it. Not that he is necessarily antagonistic to artistic merit or tries to exclude it from his production; but he is aware of the repellent quality of the word "art" for a substantial segment of the population and he knows that where box-office receipts are involved art must be bootlegged in such a way that the customers will not realize that this is what is being served up to them.

The arts, insofar as they are recognized, are believed to constitute a very special area of activity having, at best, but a tenuous relation to the activities of everyday living. On the one hand there is an actual repudiation of esthetic values—a refusal to recognize their validity as compared with "practical" values. On the other hand there is the failure to recognize as esthetic many of the experiences and activities which are a part of the life of every individual and one of his chief sources of enjoyment. It is a rare person who does not give some attention to the clothes he wears and the objects with which he surrounds himself, who is not to some degree sensitive to the superior job of photography or direction in a motion picture, or who is completely unmoved by the rhythm and coordination of a competent tennis player. But these responses are not recognized as having esthetic quality, for the artistic has been pigeonholed as a very special kind of activity and, for most people, is limited to the so-called "fine" arts.

The arts, it is true, have been subject to intense specialization no less than any other area of human endeavor. While practice in any of the arts has been, in most civilized cultures, a specialized profession, the great emphasis which our contemporary culture places on specialization and on the attainment of extreme proficiency in one small area has been an important factor in increasing the distance between the artist and the non-artist, just as it has set up barriers to communication and interchange between all highly specialized groups. There appears to be, however, another more basic reason for this lack of understanding and sympathy which afflicts both the artist and the layman. This stems from the fact that the artist, by virtue of being an artist, places the highest premium on values which have minor significance for the culture at large. By definition he is a person who puts the highest value on the esthetic aspects of reality and is devoted to the exploration and discovery of the world in terms of its esthetic meanings. To the extent that he is so oriented he is running counter to the mainstream of a culture in which scientific-materialistic values predominate. Because of this basic divergence of interests, the artist comes to be regarded as an impractical dreamer, a "queer duck," and is, quite truly, within the framework of the values which characterize our society as a whole, a social misfit.

It follows inevitably from this state of affairs that artistic ability is considered to be a very special attribute possessed only by an abnormal few. We do not regard artists in the same way that we do scientists, let us say, as individuals who have achieved more clearly the kind of vision we are all striving for. We see artists as people who have a different kind of vision, esoteric, mystical, and not to be shared by the non-artist. It is generally accepted as the normal state of affairs that a person is either artistic or inartistic and the readiness with which individuals admit complete ignorance of the arts indicates that they do not feel it to be a lack of any real consequence.

The rejection of esthetic values and the compartmentalization of the arts are thus seen to be an outgrowth of some of the most basic trends of our culture. We may ask, therefore, how the arts may best operate within such a context. Must they necessarily play such a limited and specialized role in the culture or can they make a fuller and more valuable contribution? And what is the nature of the contribution which they can make?

THE POTENTIAL ROLE OF THE ARTS
IN THE AMERICAN CULTURE

COMPENSATION FOR THE STANDARDIZATION AND SPECIALIZATION OF OUR TECHNOLOGICAL CULTURE

We have seen how the development of a machine technology and the increasing specialization of knowledge have resulted in a fragmentation of many of the activities of living and a corresponding diminution in the opportunities for whole responses, for creative action, and for integrated behavior. The close relation which the pre-industrial worker felt between his own activities and the product of his labors has been largely eliminated from modern large-scale production and the highly specialized pursuits which characterize most vocational areas today.

In almost all the other areas of our living, this same kind of fragmentation has occurred. Food, clothing, houses, entertainment, are prefabricated for us and we have little choice but to buy packaged segments of living and put them together as best we can. Our creativity is limited to making choices among the goods that are offered and combining them in the way that seems most pleasing to us. The result is a segmented kind of activity which, for the individual, has little feeling of unity or wholeness. The opportunity to view the problems of living as integrated wholes and to devise creative solutions for them has been reduced to a minimum.

In this situation the role of the arts becomes extremely important. Because art activities are essentially creative and demand integrated response and behavior, they can do much to compensate for the standardization and specialization of our mechanical society. Esthetic experience, as we have seen, derives from the perception of a situation as an integrated whole and is dependent upon the individual's affective response to relationships which he finds meaningful. Art activities, therefore, provide an invaluable means whereby the individual can search out and bring together into more integrated patterns the often disparate elements of his life.

As an example, the furnishing of a house will serve to illustrate one level, or one dimension, in which an esthetic awareness can help to integrate the individual's living. Examples are all too numerous of houses which have been furnished much in the manner that a patchwork quilt might be made. Each item of furniture is an entity in itself with only the faintest relation to the structure of the house or the other furnishings with which it shares space. In selecting the furniture, the owner has viewed each thing separately—a chair, a sofa, a bed, a table, a radio—with no attention to the relationships between one piece and another. At least as far as its physical characteristics are concerned, he has no feeling of his home as a unified whole; it is nothing more than a collection, an addition of separate and discrete parts. A greater wholeness of response—in other words, a more esthetic response—to his home as a complex of inter-related parts would give him a better basis for the selection of its furnishings and, more important, for the experiencing of his home as a place for integrated living. In the same way, esthetic sensitivity will lead to a more acute awareness of the relation between the kind of furniture one selects and the kinds of living pattern one has. An eighteenth-century living room may be beautifully unified and consistent down to the last detail but may have very little relation to the kind of living which we engage in today. Esthetic awareness will effect a closer relation between the kind of living we do and the expression of that living in the objects with which we surround ourselves. Still other relationships may be perceived between the individual's home and the community in which he lives.

This one example serves to illustrate the integrative function of esthetic sensitivity and the opportunities it provides for perceiving the wholeness of life activities. It illustrates further the fact that the relationships which are revealed to esthetic awareness are multi-dimensional and evolve into constantly expanding wholes. In much the same way that an individual can relate and integrate the furniture in his house, he can, with respect to more personal and private experiences, clarify and intensify those relationships which have the greatest significance for him and thereby attain a more integrated and unified view of life.

INCREASING UNDERSTANDING OF THE ENVIRONMENT

It has been shown how our emphasis on the scientific aspects of reality and on the material values of living has tended to blind us to the whole esthetic and emotional sphere of our environment. As we have looked at the world from only a single point of view we have seen it in but a single dimension. Furthermore, to the extent that we have been preoccupied with scientific knowledge *about* the world, we have seriously limited our knowledge *of* the world, for we have gained little more than a collection of cold facts whose only value is an extrinsic one. In addition, the tendency to view things purely as practical means to practical ends blinds us to all aspects of the environment save those which have some value for the realization of these ends.

Esthetic vision, on the other hand, has no end other than the experience itself and its value is not in the attainment of some outside goal but in the richness of the experience. It brings with it a curiosity about the world and a desire to experience it more fully for its own sake. Therefore it opens up to the individual new ways of seeing and perceiving the world, enriching his experience and enlarging his values.

In addition to an increased sensitivity to the physical environment, esthetic awareness can also reveal new aspects of the social and cultural environment. This takes on added importance as specialization increases because, as we have seen, this particular aspect of our culture induces a narrow and biased view of life, and it becomes increasingly difficult to get outside ourselves for a larger view of the world in which we live. Furthermore, there are certain aspects of the environment which can be experienced in no other way because the arts are the only means for communicating them. Read, in the following quotation, emphasizes the role of the arts in increasing social understanding and integration:

As individuals we create to communicate: We create a language out of sounds, we create a pictorial language out of line and color. But every language, even the language of art, is a communal creation; it represents an agreed upon system of signs to be used in common. Art is a bond. It is not a bond which should be the exclusive privilege of a class, of a tiny group of connoisseurs and artists. Art should be an integral part of our communal life, as it was in Ancient Greece, as it was in the Middle Ages: it should enter our lives at the formative stage, as a natural function of human relationships, as the language of form and color, as universal and innocent as the language of words.[13]

Learning the language of art can give us deeper insights, not only into our own cultural group, but also into other cultures in the present world and the cultures of our historic past. As we try desperately to recover from a second world conflict and to avoid a third and possibly last one, we must use every resource at our command to learn what the past has to give us and to increase human understanding among men today.

PROVISION OF CREATIVE LEISURE-TIME ACTIVITIES

One of the potential values of our technology is the continuing decrease in the length of the average working day and the corresponding increase in leisure time. This is called a potential value because it constitutes a real challenge to our society, and to education in particular, whether or not the use of this leisure time can be directed into productive and rewarding channels. Today the tendency toward standardization and specialization has permeated the area of leisure-time activities as it has every other aspect of our living. Most of our entertainment today is mass-produced by highly trained specialists for consumption by a passive audience. Instead of playing baseball we go to watch the Red Sox and the Dodgers; instead of singing with a neighborhood group we prefer to go to the Metropolitan Opera to hear a highly professional performance. Radio, television, and motion pictures represent the kinds of entertainment most widely sought after by the American public. Excellent as these forms of entertainment may sometimes be, they present the very serious problem that they offer no opportunity for active participation on the part of the audience. The kind of intellectual, emotional, and physical lethargy which such passivity induces can hardly be overestimated as a threat to the maintenance

[13] Herbert Read, *The Grass Roots of Art* (New York: Wittenborn, Schultz, Inc., 1949), p. 62.

of a vigorous intellectual and artistic life in our culture—indeed, as a threat to the democratic way of life.

There are those who deplore the recent increase in the number of "Sunday painters" on the ground that their efforts can have little, if any, artistic merit, and that it is a kind of artistic treason to encourage such "dabbling." This same general attitude may be felt with respect to amateur participation in any of the arts, but the current surge of interest in the pictorial arts has elicited particularly strong criticisms in that field. That few works of real artistic merit will be produced by these amateur artists may be entirely true, but this seems to be somewhat beside the point. The real value of such activity seems to lie rather in the sense of fulfillment and accomplishment which the amateur derives from it and the opportunity which it provides for the heightening and clarification of his own emotional and intuitive perceptions.

There is also another argument against the criticisms which are leveled at amateur performance in the arts. Such activities have great possibilities for narrowing the gulf which exists between the layman and the professional in the arts. The sharp separation and the misunderstanding and distrust which exist today between the artist and the layman are serious deterrents to a healthy cultural development. The greatest artistic achievements emanate from a broad base of interest and activity and the great masterpiece is the culmination, the highest expression, of such activity. It seems, therefore, that a more widespread participation in artistic activities offers one hope for effecting a closer integration between the artist and society.

A REORIENTATION OF VALUES: POINTING
TOWARD SOCIAL RECONSTRUCTION

Much of the foregoing discussion has dealt with the contributions which the arts might make toward compensating for some of the lacks and the inadequacies of our present cultural patterns. To stop at this point, therefore, would be to imply that there is actually no way of reconciling our technology with the individual's needs for full esthetic experience and that the role of the arts is simply to act as an antidote to the evils of a culture the basic character of which we are powerless to change.

Properly conceived, the awakening of esthetic awareness can and should play an important part in the reconstruction of our culture. Individuals tend to evaluate a culture in terms of how well it satisfies the conditions for what they believe to be a full life, and in a democratic culture social forms are revised in accordance with the values of the group. Our first and most important task, therefore, is to arouse in people an awareness of esthetic values and of the potentialities of creative activity in terms of human development and human satisfaction. As they perceive the validity of esthetic experience and as the need for creative activity becomes a conscious need, this reorientation will lead to a reevaluation of the culture and, through democratic processes, to the evolution of social forms more fully conceived in terms of rich and meaningful human living.

Part Three

ART
IN THE COLLEGE PROGRAM
OF GENERAL EDUCATION

Chapter VII

CURRENT TRENDS IN COLLEGE ART COURSES

GROWING RECOGNITION OF THE IMPORTANCE OF THE ARTS

In general the arts have received but scant attention in higher education in the United States. For the most part they have been considered unnecessary, though perhaps graceful, embellishments to an education; but only in rare instances have they been considered essential to a complete education. This state of affairs has been more or less prevalent at all levels of education but it is probably at the college level that it has been most marked. In the elementary grades, the arts, while not enjoying the same status as the academic subjects, are recognized, at least in many school systems, as being a part of the regular curriculum. To a lesser degree, this is also true in the high school. It is but recently that the arts have gained comparable status in colleges, and this only in rare cases.

In spite of this generally bleak picture, developments in recent years have indicated a growing recognition of the importance of the arts and the need for giving them a more prominent place in higher education. The results of a survey made by Goldwater[1] show significant gains in the number of courses offered by colleges during the period from 1900 to 1940. The survey included fifty colleges scattered throughout the United States; eleven of them were men's colleges, ten were women's colleges, and twenty-nine were coeducational. The survey deals separately with the four following types of courses: introductory courses which either give a survey of the visual arts in a chronological sequence or are organized around the analysis of great works of art and in which there is no studio experience provided; art history courses; introductory studio courses; and studio courses.

The results show that in 1900 only thirty of the forty-eight colleges then in existence offered any courses in art history, and of these only eight offered a general introductory course. By 1940 such introductory courses were given by forty-one out of the fifty colleges in the study. Also by this date all of the colleges in the study gave some courses in art history, the total number of courses offered being 795; and in thirty-nine of the colleges it was possible for students to take a major in art history.

The data provided for introductory studio and studio courses are not as complete, but they do show that in 1900 there were no colleges in the group which offered introductory studio courses, while in 1940 fifteen out of the fifty had such a course. The total number of studio courses given in 1940 was over 1000, although in eight of the fifty colleges no work of this kind was provided. Particular mention is made of the fact that of the eastern men's colleges studied, five gave no work at all in the studio and the rest "made no real attempt at any rounded sort of training within the undergraduate years."

The table which follows, based on the report of the study, shows some indication of the increase in art instruction which has taken place.

Another study, conducted by Bobbitt, deals with forty-two liberal arts colleges "which were, for the most part, church-related, coeducational and which normally enrolled not more

[1] Robert J. Goldwater, "Teaching of Art in the Colleges of the United States," *College Art Journal*, Supplement II (May, 1943), 31 pp.

Number and Distribution of Art Teachers in Fifty American Colleges, 1900–1940

Year	Total Teachers		History Teachers		Studio Teachers		Teaching Both	
	Number	Percent Increase over 1900	Number	Percent Increase over 1900	Number	Percent Increase over 1900	Number	Percent Increase over 1900
1900	114		43		55		16	
1910	174	53	69	60	74	35	31	94
1920	230	102	90	109	95	73	45	181
1930	353	210	140	226	154	180	59	269
1940	454	298	172	300	202	267	80	400

From Goldwater, *op. cit.*, p. 31.

than 1500 students." [2] The study compares course offerings and requirements, number of teachers, and enrollments, for the academic years 1941–42 and 1946–47. Of the forty-two colleges replying to the questionnaire on which the study is based, there were seven which had no art department and offered no art instruction of any kind. Probably the most significant figures in the study are those dealing with student enrollment. In the thirty-five colleges offering art courses, the increase in total enrollment from 1941–42 to 1946–47 was from 19,989 to 34,041, a gain of approximately seventy per cent. During the same period, the enrollment in art courses went from 2,642 students to 5,054, an increase of ninety per cent. One of the most significant aspects of these figures is to be found in the fact that in only two of the colleges was an art course listed as a requirement for the bachelor's degree, although twelve of them required that at least one course be selected from the art, music, philosophy, or drama departments for graduation. It may be assumed, therefore, that this increase, for the most part, represents a voluntary movement on the part of the students.

While these two studies are far from conclusive, they do offer substantial evidence of a trend of major proportion toward a recognition of the arts as a valid and valuable part of the college program. It is important to remember that the study by Goldwater goes only to 1940 and Bobbitt's study is now five years old. The growth which they record has, if anything, accelerated in more recent years and similar studies today would undoubt-

[2] Unpublished study by Vernon Bobbitt, Director of Art, Albion College.

edly reveal even more striking gains. However, numerical increase is only one aspect of the total picture; in order properly to assess the gains which have been made it is necessary to look further at some of the dominant patterns which have characterized college offerings in art.

DOMINANCE OF THE INTELLECTUAL APPROACH IN COLLEGE ART COURSES

One of the most frequent and most influential arguments against recognizing the arts as a valid part of the college curriculum has been the idea that the college, as an institution for the pursuit of intellectual ends, would betray its function by doing so. Because of this emphasis on intellectualism, there has been a marked tendency to admit the arts into the college program only as they could be converted into intellectual disciplines comparable to the disciplines of logic, or mathematics, or the natural sciences. The most striking result of this need to intellectualize all the offerings of the college has been a predominance of the historical approach in the study of the arts. With respect to this situation, Longman has commented as follows:

There are . . . instances where only historical studies in the fine arts are allowed in the curriculum of the college, studio work being disqualified as "technical" rather than liberal. This . . . results from a fundamental misunderstanding of the nature of the fine arts, surprising when it appears in one who knows their history. The argument appears to be that the university is an "intellectual" institution, and that the creative process in the arts is inherently technical in the sense of a trade or a craft, demanding little of either knowledge or wit, and supplementing the methodical only by flights of fancy or emotional effervescence. It is a judgment apparently deriving from observing the lowest forms of expression in the arts rather than the highest. Obviously, Leonardo da Vinci would not agree, nor do the educators who hold this thesis ascribe such limitations to leading painters, architects, and sculptors of the past.[3]

This state of affairs is reflected in figures from the study by Goldwater cited above. It will be remembered that of the fifty colleges studied only fifteen offered introductory studio courses whereas forty-one offered introductory courses in history or

[3] In McGrath and others, *op. cit.*, p. 189.

appreciation. It may also be of significance that of the fifteen, ten were coeducational colleges in the South and the Midwest; this would seem to indicate that the newer colleges are having somewhat less difficulty in breaking away from traditional attitudes toward the inclusion of studio work in college art courses than are the older institutions in the East.

The field of esthetics, sometimes as a branch of philosophy and sometimes as an area of psychological investigation, has also enjoyed some prestige in the college program. Here again, however, the approach is almost exclusively intellectual; courses are devoted to discussion and comparison of various theories of esthetics and their philosophical and metaphysical implications, or to an investigation of the psychobiological factors involved in the esthetic experience. In many such courses there is little, if any, actual contact with works of art—much less with artistic expression. They are not so much concerned that students should have an esthetic experience as that they should acquire an intellectual understanding of esthetic theories. The writer well remembers a college course in esthetics in which the only works of art used as illustrative material during the entire course were a small vase and a cold-cream jar. There is the story too of the German esthetician who, in a letter to William James, wrote that he was passionately interested in the subject of esthetics, but as for works of music or poetry he found them extremely dull. Esthetics endeavors primarily to arrive at an intellectual understanding of the art experience much as the biologist dissects a frog in order to understand its life processes. Such understanding may be extremely important but it is no substitute for the experience of art itself.

The distinctive values of the art experience are thus largely ignored in a considerable proportion of college art courses. Offerings in art history or in esthetics differ from offerings in other subject areas only in the sense that they provide the student with information in another field of organized knowledge. The experience which the student has is still largely an intellectual one, and in this sense is not to be distinguished from activity in any other area. With respect to the statement by Longman which is quoted above, it is interesting to note that even though it is a strong argument in favor of the inclusion of studio work in college instruction, it defends such activity on the ground that it too has an intellectual component. A much more persuasive argument would seem to be that such activity is essentially emotional and intuitive and thereby has a unique contribution to make to the student's growth and development. It is the failure to recognize the importance of this kind of experience in human living which is primarily responsible for the neglect of the arts in the college program, and for the very heavy emphasis on an intellectual approach in much of the work which the college has offered. Whatever intellectual values there may be in the study of the arts, whether in art history, appreciation, esthetics, or studio work, art courses which justify their existence solely on the basis of their value as intellectual disciplines are side-stepping the unique, and the most important, contribution which the arts can make to human living.

TENDENCIES TOWARD PROFESSIONALISM

Much of the instruction which has been provided by colleges in art, as well as in other fields, has been poorly suited to the needs and interests of the general student for it has been structured primarily for the student with special interests and vocational objectives in the arts. In a great many cases there has been no distinction between the specialist and the non-specialist in art offerings and students who are interested in the arts as a part of a general or liberal education have had no choice but to take introductory or beginning work which has been designed to launch the specialist on a protracted course of study. For a student who can devote but a limited amount of his program to the arts, a course dealing only with life drawing or watercolor painting or clay modeling is far from satisfactory because it touches such a limited area of the total field. The same may be said of a course which is devoted exclusively to a historical or theoretical treatment of the arts. The situation would be somewhat less unfortunate if such courses, even narrowed down as they are, gave more consideration to the needs of the general student, but as McGrath has said, "Even institutions which make no attempt to educate professional artists offer courses which reflect the narrow interests of the historian or the theorist and deal with detailed and technical subject matter of little interest and value to the future doctor, lawyer, social worker, or businessman." [4]

While it is true that there may be a substantial number of general students whose interests have perhaps become focused on some particular aspect of the arts and who thus derive considerable benefit from such courses, their needs are only partially met in courses with a highly professional and technical orientation. Furthermore, there is the much larger group of students whose interests have not been narrowed to a single aspect of the arts and who can be adequately served only by instruction of a much more general nature. The specialization and the emphasis on highly professional interests and standards which typify such a large percentage of college art instruction can be nothing more than a poor second-best for such students.

LIMITATION OF SUBJECT MATTER
TO THE FINE ARTS

Largely as a result of the specialization and professionalism of college offerings in art, instruction has been limited almost exclusively to the fine arts—painting, sculpture, and architecture—with sometimes scant attention being given to such minor arts as pottery and weaving. Within the field of the fine arts, furthermore, a disproportionate amount of attention has been given to painting as compared with sculpture and architecture. The previously mentioned study by Goldwater shows that of the art history courses surveyed there were twice as many courses in painting as in architecture and sculpture combined.

The result of such limitations is to reinforce the already prevalent conviction that art is a thing apart from life. The inexperienced student with little or no background in the fine arts, if he is plunged headlong into a study of the great masterpieces of painting, sculpture, and architecture, may often wonder how these relate to the pursuits of his daily life. He is thus forced

[4] Earl J. McGrath, "The Fine Arts in General Education," *Art Education Organizes,* 1949 Yearbook of the National Art Education Association (Kutztown: The Association, 1949), p. 41.

to pay a double penalty: the potentialities for esthetic experience in his daily living are not realized, and his understanding and appreciation of the fine arts are hampered because he has difficulty in relating them to his own experiences.

EMPHASIS ON HISTORIC PERIODS OF ART

Referring again to the study by Goldwater, we find evidence of a heavy overweighting in favor of the historic periods of art as compared with the contemporary arts. The following table, which has been adapted from the study, shows that although there has been a slight proportional gain in courses dealing with modern art during the forty-year period surveyed, the emphasis on historic periods is still disproportionately heavy.

Distribution of Courses in Art History in Fifty American Colleges, 1900–1940

	1900		1910		1920		1930		1940	
	No.	% of Total	No.	% of Total	No.	% of Total	No.	% of Total	No.	% of Total
Classical	75	64.9	120	61.5	103	46.0	94	32.3	128	28.4
Medieval	15	13.0	28	14.4	34	15.2	55	18.9	107	23.8
Renaissance	23	20.0	38	19.5	55	24.5	85	29.2	104	23.1
Baroque	½	0.4	3	1.5	13	5.8	32	11.0	56	12.4
Modern	2	1.7	6	3.1	19	8.5	25	8.6	55	12.2
Total	115½	100.0	195	100.0	224	100.0	291	100.0	450	99.9

From Goldwater, *op. cit.*, p. 31.

It should be further noted that even those courses which purport to deal with the complete span of the arts in Western civilization end, through poor timing and the temptation to linger over historic periods, by giving no more than the scantest attention to the contemporary arts. In describing the way in which this occurs, MacMahon has written, "Usually during the Periclean age the teacher is still fairly relaxed; halfway through the Roman period he notes that mid-semester is approaching; at the end of the Renaissance he becomes frankly alarmed by *tempus fugit*, with the result that he races through modern times at a truly breath-taking speed." [5] It is this type of historical survey

[5] D. H. MacMahon, "A New Approach to the Humanities," *Journal of Higher Education*, XVII (November, 1946), 417.

course which is generally recommended to the non-specialist student since many of the courses dealing exclusively with the modern arts assume a prior background of historical study. As a result of these factors it frequently happens that the student comes away having had little if any contact with the art of his own time.

RECENT TRENDS TOWARD A GENERAL EDUCATION VIEW OF ART INSTRUCTION

Along with the negative aspects of college art instruction which have been noted in the preceding pages, there are many developments of a more encouraging nature. In an increasing number of colleges attempts are being made to provide instruction in the arts which is geared specifically to the needs and interests of young people whose major concerns are with other fields of endeavor. These efforts have resulted in many different approaches and types of courses, some more successful than others. Emerging from the total pattern are a number of trends which are of major importance.

First to be noted is the fact that in the formulation of general courses much greater attention is being paid to the particular needs and interests of the students whom they are designed to serve. While there may be considerable disagreement as to the manner in which student needs are conceived and the kinds of experiences deemed most suitable to meet those needs, the greatest gain is in the fact that attention *is* being focused on the needs of students, and subject matter has been at least partially displaced as the *raison d'être* of instruction.

The tendency to utilize the interests of students as the motivation for specific learning activities is perhaps most marked in studio courses where the students are actually engaged in creative activities. Studio procedures based on the assignment of specific problems are gradually giving way to a freer kind of situation in which students, with the help of the instructor, work on problems of their own choosing in line with their particular interests. While student participation in the planning of activities is still comparatively rare in the lecture and discussion type of course, there is a growing recognition of the importance of such procedures and efforts are being made in many instances to facilitate student planning.

A particular aspect of the increased emphasis on student needs and interests is a greater attention to the arts in contemporary living. This is evident in several ways. In the first place, there is an increasing tendency to move beyond the traditional boundaries of the fine arts and to give fuller consideration to art forms more closely related to the daily life of the average student such as commercial and industrial art, city planning, domestic architecture, and interior design. For example, "Art Today," the course offered in the General College at the University of Minnesota, deals with the arts as they relate to various areas of contemporary living: religion, the home, the community, industry, commerce, and so forth. Courses such as this not only deal more fully with those art forms which are part of the life of every student; they are also organized specifically in terms of the students' life activities. Along with this trend toward a broader treatment of the arts, there is also evidence that in the treatment of the fine arts considerably greater emphasis is being placed on the work of contemporary artists who are part of the same world in which the students themselves are living. This shift in emphasis in no sense implies a denial of the value of historic arts; it is based rather on the belief that through an understanding and appreciation of the artistic expression which is an integral part of his own cultural environment, the student will be helped to more direct and penetrating insights into his own life and the world in which he lives.

In many instances efforts have been made to break down the barriers which have so long separated the various forms of artistic expression—the visual arts, music, dance, drama, and literature. There have been many examples of correlated activities involving the visual arts and another form such as music or poetry. Dramatic productions have frequently provided the core around which activities in drama, music, and the visual arts have been coordinated. There are also an increasing number of survey courses in which several of the major art forms are studied and their basic similarities as well as their differences provide the unifying element of the course. For example, the Humanities course at Stephens College has been described as comprising "the five major arts: painting, sculpture, architecture, literature, and music with secondary emphasis on the applied arts: ceramics, weaving, metalwork, and the combined arts: the theatre, the opera, and the cinema." [6] And the General Arts course in the General College of the University of Minnesota is "designed to show the student interested in music, the plastic and graphic arts, the dramatic arts, or literature how his favorite art is closely related to the other arts." [7]

Many courses in the humanities not only emphasize the interrelationships between the arts but also treat them in relation to the entire social and cultural context. Thus, the Humanities course at the University of Minnesota uses as its organizing idea "man and the everchanging conception of himself, his relations with his fellow men, and his methods of regulating human affairs." [8] However, it is not only in the humanities that such tendencies may be noted. The organization of "Art Today," described above, is designed to illuminate the relationships between the arts and the other strands of our social fabric. Instruction in the history of art is, in many cases, giving increasing attention to the social origins of artistic expression. "The Language of Visual Art," which is the basic course in art at Bennington College, provides an example in which, although a historic sequence is followed, the primary emphasis is on the philosophical, social, and economic forces which have been influential in shaping the artistic achievements of various cultural epochs. According to the catalog statement, this course endeavors, among other things, "to induce an awareness of the relation between visual art and significant epochs of culture" and to help the student "to draw conclusions from . . . analysis as to the driving forces behind the creative change which a work of art represents." [9] In all of

[6] Marjorie K. Carpenter, "The Humanities Course at Stephens College," *College Art Journal*, II (November, 1942), 11.

[7] University of Minnesota, "The General College," *The Bulletin of the University of Minnesota*, LII (July 6, 1949), 20.

[8] Laurence Schmeckebier, "Humanities in the Modern World," *College Art Journal*, II (March, 1943), 77.

[9] Bennington College, "Announcement for the Year," *Bennington College Bulletin*, XIX (July, 1950), 59.

these instances, the purpose is to provide a broader basis for an understanding and appreciation of the arts in order that the student may see them in a more meaningful relation to the total fabric of living.

Probably one of the most important developments to be noted is the increasing recognition of the importance of studio work in art for the general student. Although the data provided by Goldwater are far from conclusive, they show that in 1940 the fifty colleges studied offered over 1000 studio courses in art as compared with 795 courses in art history. While the great majority of these courses were for students specializing in art, the figures are significant in that they indicate the growing importance of studio work in the total college art program. Against these figures must be balanced the ones quoted earlier which showed that there were only fifteen introductory studio courses as compared with forty-one introductory courses in history and appreciation. It is to be remembered, however, that these figures represent the situation as it existed in 1940, and comparable figures for 1950 would no doubt show a substantial increase in studio offerings for the general student, for the impetus which such work has received in the past ten years has been considerable.

In assessing the total situation, we may conclude first of all that there is a constantly growing interest in the arts and an increased recognition that they constitute a legitimate part of the college program. In much of the work which is offered there is an excessive emphasis on intellectualism and a consequent denial of the unique contributions which the arts can make to the education of students. Many courses are also characterized by specialization and professionalism and by an overweighting in favor of historic arts which make them poorly adapted to the needs of general students. On the other hand, as a part of the total development in general education there is a significant movement toward the revision and enlargement of art offerings to meet the needs of these young people in order, first, that they will be assured some experience in the arts as a part of their general education and also that such experience as they do have will be of maximum significance in their lives. Against this background, and in the light of the discussion in the two preceding parts, the remainder of the study will be devoted to a consideration of the purposes of art instruction in the college program of general education and the major problems involved in implementing a program built on these purposes.

Chapter VIII

BROAD PURPOSES OF THE ART PROGRAM IN GENERAL EDUCATION

In Part One of this study general education was presented as being primarily concerned with developing the student's potentialities for a rich and satisfying life both as an individual and as a member of society. It was distinguished on the one hand from special education which is concerned with competency in some vocation, and on the other hand from uniform education which disregards the uniqueness of human personalities. Within the framework of that earlier discussion we may ask how the arts will best contribute to the realization of the over-all purposes of general education. What are the purposes of an art program which will be of maximum value in helping to achieve the larger aims of general education?

The first purpose of such a program would be *to provide opportunities for the development of the individual's creative potentialities and to foster genuinely creative expression in the arts.* The importance of this aim derives from several factors. We have seen, in the first place, that every individual has the need and the capacity for creative action. Indeed, it is only through such action that he is able to integrate the otherwise disparate and disconnected facets of his life and to achieve a sense of selfhood. It has also been pointed out how a number of factors in contemporary life have seriously limited the opportunities for creative action in the daily pursuits of living and how, furthermore, the individual, feeling alone and insecure in the midst of a vast and complex social organization, tends to retreat into stereotyped patterns of behavior, thus sacrificing his selfhood for a sense—though it be a false sense—of security and belongingness.

In this state of affairs, creative activity in the arts assumes a role of major importance, for as the individual's opportunities for such activity in his daily pursuits become increasingly limited, participation in the arts takes on added significance. One of the first tasks of education in the arts is to awaken in individuals a feeling for the importance and the necessity of creative action as an indispensable element of full and rounded living. This, moreover, may frequently prove to be a most difficult task, for the pressures toward conformity which are present in our contemporary cultural patterns are such as to suppress the natural human urge for free, spontaneous behavior, and the first reactions of many students may be to shrink from the opportunity for such activity rather than to welcome it.

A further reason for the primacy of this purpose in the art program is the fact that creative activity in the arts is the only means whereby certain aspects of emotional and intuitive experience can be adequately brought to full realization and expression. It has been a widely held concept that whereas nearly all people have the capacity for appreciation of the arts only a limited number have any capacity for artistic creation. The point of view which is basic to the purpose stated here is that all individuals, to the extent that they have a life of emotion and feeling, have both the need and the capacity, to some degree, to express this life in artistic form. Furthermore, their development as human personalities cannot be fully realized unless they can express this aspect of their lives through the experience of creative activity in the arts.

It is important to note here that emphasis is placed on the individual's creative experience rather than on the objects which he creates, on *process* rather than on *product*. It is the failure to recognize this emphasis which has been responsible for much of the criticism leveled against amateur participation in art activities. Such criticism is generally based on the fact that the work produced, when judged by professional standards, is frequently of inferior quality; the emotional growth and development of the individual which result from such activities are overlooked. A typical criticism runs as follows:

As for . . . survey courses in the practice of the arts . . . I can conceive of their producing, not even Sunday painters, not even creditable amateurs, but only the painting and sculpture equivalents of poetasters, the most contemptuous word in the language, and properly so. Better an outright critic who doesn't try to draw a straight line than the dilettante who thinks he can paint a watercolor. A survey course in the practice of surgery would not be more harmful. In short, let us drink deep or not taste.[1]

This application of professional standards to the work of the non-specialist seems to overlook entirely the fact that these *are* amateur painters and sculptors and designers with whom we are working, and that the criteria which are applied to their products must be adjusted to this important fact. The value of their activity is not to be judged in terms of its professional quality but rather in terms of how much it has contributed to their emotional development, their personal integration, and their keener perception of the world in which they live.

Another important value of creative activity in the arts is the contribution which it makes to a fuller understanding and appreciation of the arts themselves. Washburn has written, "Those interested in the teaching of creative arts believe that the creative process has not changed since the beginning of time and of art; that an understanding of the process is essential to the fullest appreciation of art and life; that such understanding is most fully realized through practice. . . ."[2]

[1] Phillip R. Adams, "Fine Arts in Liberal Education," *Association of American Colleges Bulletin*, XXXIV (May, 1948), 240–41.
[2] Helen P. Washburn, "Creative Arts and Higher Education," *Association of American Colleges Bulletin*, XXX (December, 1944), 553.

In support of this same point of view, Mursell has written as follows:

[Artistic production] is *par excellence* the process in and through which one learns to perceive the possibilities of beauty, and proceeds to work them out. The nine symphonies of Beethoven are the landmarks of his own inner development as a seer of beauty—the stages in his aesthetic education. The productive endeavors of a child [or, equally, of a college student], when properly understood, guided, and encouraged, are in just the same sense, stages in his aesthetic education. That is why one learns more about pictorial art by painting pictures, even bad ones, than by just looking at them— why one learns more about the true inwardness of music by composing music, even very crudely, than by just listening to it or playing it.[3]

It is undoubtedly true that a very rich appreciation of the arts is possible without any background of actual practice; indeed there are many cases in which individuals who have had no practical experience in the arts are more sensitive than others who have engaged in creative activity. This, however, does not change the basic fact that through actual experience the individual gains a deeper and clearer insight into the problems and the methods of creative activity and thereby broadens his basis for appreciation. As Walt Whitman has said, "To have great poets there must be great audiences too."[4] Creative activity, by refining and deepening the individual's esthetic perception, can contribute to the building of a greater audience for historic arts as well as for the arts of the present day.

The second purpose of the arts in general education is *to develop an understanding of the validity of esthetic experience and the capacity for esthetic response*. With respect to this purpose, Mursell has written as follows:

It is not so much with the arts as such, as specific disciplines each with a long tradition and an elaborate set of techniques, that the average citizen is concerned in his daily doings. Rather it is *beauty* with which he is concerned—beauty in its many modes, beauty in tone, in visual arrangements, in words, in images, in bodily movement, in sequences and patterns of ideas, beauty in his home, his

[3] James L. Mursell, "The Arts in American Education," *Educational Forum*, VIII (January, 1944), 153.
[4] Quoted in Helen P. Washburn, *op. cit.*, p. 557.

community, his work-place, his recreations. What he needs is not so much to become an amateur of this or that art, but an amateur of beauty. . . .

Here is our educational clue. The clear implication is to think in terms of a broad, unified segment of human education which, to use a German term which has never gained popularity in this country, may be called aesthetic education—whose central purpose is to promote responsiveness to the manifold aesthetic values and manifestations which our civilization is throwing into such high relief.[5]

It is a shortcoming of many courses in art that they become so preoccupied with a specific segment of the field as to overlook almost completely the broader implications of a basically esthetic attitude toward experience. In studio courses, for example, the techniques of art may be so emphasized that the esthetic experience is largely neglected. This is abundantly true in many art history courses, and even in esthetics courses which are more concerned that students should gain a theoretical understanding of the subject than that they should have a deeply felt esthetic experience. In our present culture, with its great emphasis on scientific and material values, it is of particular importance that students should be able, through direct experience, to achieve an understanding of esthetic reality and to see its importance for rich and balanced living.

The third purpose of the arts in general education is closely related to the preceding one and may be stated as follows: *to foster esthetic evaluation of all aspects of the environment and to encourage the disposition to act in accordance with such evaluation.* It is a common occurrence in education that learnings become so pigeonholed and compartmentalized that they are rarely, if ever, applied to actual life situations. The story of the physics major who was at a loss when faced with the problem of prying a lid off a crate with a crow-bar is a classic example of the separation between academic learning and life situations. The same phenomenon is all too common with respect to learning in the arts. This was the case with the German esthetician referred to earlier whose only interest in his subject was abstract and academic and who was apathetic to actual works of art. It is essential therefore that education in the arts give specific atten-

[5] Mursell, *op. cit.*, p. 152.

tion to the development of an esthetic attitude which the student will carry into his daily living.

It should be noted that esthetic criteria are to be applied to *all* aspects of the environment. It seems clear that such criteria cannot, and should not, be the dominant ones in every situation. Practical considerations obviously make this both impossible and undesirable. Furthermore, Northrop's concept of the "spectrum of aesthetic possibilities" (pp. 73–74) makes it clear that the very nature of many experiences eliminates the possibility for all but a minimum of the esthetic factor. On the other hand, there is in every life situation, to some degree, an esthetic element, and even the most practical experiences and activities have some potentialities for an esthetic organization, or, by virtue of their organization—even though directed toward purely practical ends—they present possibilities for esthetic enjoyment. It is the purpose of the art program to illuminate the relevance of esthetic criteria to the entire fabric of life and to encourage students to apply them as they have relevance.

One further step is necessary for the full realization of the esthetic values of living, and this is the disposition to act in accordance with one's esthetic evaluations. It is one thing to be repelled by the litter and disorganization of a congested urban area; it is another thing to take active steps for its improvement. Similarly, an individual may be enthusiastic about community plans for the development of an art center, but unless he participates actively in helping to bring it into existence his enthusiasm is of little avail. It was stated in Chapter III that the final test of any education is the behavior which results from it. This is no less true in the arts than in any other field. Unless education in the arts brings about behavior patterns which are consistent with, and which demonstrate, an esthetic approach to the many facets of living, it can hardly be said to have succeeded in the realization of this objective.

The fourth purpose of the art program in general education is *to enrich and deepen the individual's experience of the world in which he lives through an understanding of contemporary art forms.* Our culture presents the situation in which the average individual is more sympathetic to the artistic productions of earlier civilizations not his own than to those arts which have developed out of the environment in which he lives. This can be explained at least partially on the basis of greater familiarity with historic arts. Of equal importance is the fact that great artists in any period move ahead of their times just as do great scientists and philosophers, and the layman demands time and sympathetic understanding to allow him to catch up, so to speak. All too often, however, our schools have rejected the contemporary arts almost as completely as the layman and thus, instead of helping him to a fuller understanding and appreciation, have strengthened his prejudices and made him more resistant.

For the individual whose perceptions and sympathies have been awakened to contemporary artistic expression it can be a most valuable means to a richer and fuller understanding of himself and the world in which he lives. It is certainly true that the expressions of many contemporary artists are exceedingly difficult for the layman because the artist is pushing back the boundaries of esthetic vision and is charting unexplored territory. This is especially true in our own time because of the general esthetic illiteracy of the culture at large. These facts only increase the importance of the contemporary arts in the education of the student for they have the greatest potentialities for giving him new ways of seeing and perceiving the world and deepening his insights into contemporary living. In speaking of the role of the artist in helping to shape the future, Mac-Murray has written as follows:

. . . we shall have to attend to the artists, and learn how to attend. And it is the modern artists that we must look to in our need; the old masters are useless. They have no knowledge of the actual world in which we live, out of which a new world might be created. The craze for what is old and what has stood the appraisal of the centuries is a symptom of the fear of art rather than of the love of it. The cult of the antique may develop taste, but it tends to destroy artistic receptivity. For the old has done its work of social transformation. It remains as a monument of beauty. But a living work of art strikes always at the roots of our complacency and its beauty is hidden by its attack upon our security and our traditions.[6]

[6] John MacMurray, *Reason and Emotion*, pp. 167–68. Copyright, 1938, D. Appleton-Century Company, Inc.

This statement does much to explain both the resistance which the average person frequently feels toward contemporary art and the rich rewards which it offers once the resistance has been overcome. If the student's initial prejudices can be dislodged, the art of his own times can be the richest source for re-experiencing his own world, for it deals, albeit in often unfamiliar terms, with the things which are happening today and is motivated by experiences which are surely closer to his own life than were the experiences of a Greek sculptor or a Medieval craftsman. And, as MacMurray suggests, it not only helps him toward a fuller understanding of the world as it is but also toward a vision of the world as it might be. The least which education can do is to foster an attitude of tolerance and open-mindedness toward contemporary expression in the arts, thus giving the student a sound basis for further exploration and enjoyment and a desire to enlarge his experience through fuller understanding.

The fifth purpose of the art program in general education is *to increase the individual's understanding of past cultures and their contributions to contemporary culture through an appreciation of the arts of the past.* In addition to their potentialities for purely esthetic experience, the chief contribution of the historic arts is in giving the student a fuller understanding of contemporary life by providing a broader perspective and allowing him to see the contemporary world in its relation to past cultures. It seems that this is the sense in which the passage quoted above from MacMurray is to be interpreted; the arts, as he has indicated, provide the most eloquent evidence of the values and the aspirations of the culture in which they were produced, and since cultural development is an evolutionary process, the roots of our present civilization extend far back into history. While the historic arts do not deal directly with the world of today, they do provide a context in which our present cultural forms can be more adequately understood.

It does not follow necessarily, however, that a knowledge of history will increase our understanding of the present world. When history is studied as an end in itself, the only result is that the student acquires a knowledge of history. Only as historical study is geared to an understanding of contemporary life will it make a significant contribution to such understanding. In the study of the historic arts, therefore, particular emphasis should be placed on their relevance to the life in which we engage today—the way in which our culture has evolved from the cultures of the past, the persistent patterns which have given continuity to the development, and the manner in which new conditions and new modes of living serve to distinguish us from earlier periods. Studied in relation to the total cultural context and with particular reference to contemporary life, the historic arts can make a valuable contribution to the student's concept of himself and his world.

Chapter IX

PROBLEMS OF PLANNING

RELATING ART INSTRUCTION TO THE TOTAL GENERAL EDUCATION PROGRAM

With respect to the place of the arts in the college curriculum, McGrath has said that "In many universities . . . such instruction is organically and spiritually separated from the other divisions of the academic community." [1] In all fairness it should be stated that this is a situation which is by no means peculiar to the arts. As college instruction has become more diversified and specialized each department has tended to become isolated from all the others. The isolation of the arts has perhaps been somewhat more complete because they have only rarely enjoyed the status of full membership in the academic community.

The most unfortunate result of such separatism has been the disjointed character of the educational fare which has been offered to students. The cafeteria system of education has re-

[1] Earl J. McGrath, "The Fine Arts in General Education," *Art Education Organizes,* 1949 Yearbook of the National Art Education Association (Kutztown: The Association, 1949), pp. 39–40.

sulted, in most cases, in a sampling of unrelated bits of subject matter and knowledge, and it has been up to the student to do what he could on his own to bring these disparate elements into some kind of a unified whole. The problem of relating art instruction to the total general education program is therefore only part of the larger problem of building a general education program which is unified in all its parts.

The first condition for effecting a closer relationship between the arts and the rest of the college program is a full recognition of the importance of art experience in the education of the student. In the past one of the chief difficulties has frequently been that educators themselves have failed to understand the significance of art experience for full and satisfying living. It should be added that this lack of vision and understanding has not been limited to educators in other fields but, in all too many cases, has characterized teachers in the arts whose vision has been distorted by narrow specialization. So long as the arts are regarded by the college itself as having little relation or relevance to the student's life, and art instruction is relegated to a place of minor importance, there can be little hope that such instruction will be meaningfully related to the student's other educational experiences. Only as the arts are recognized as being essential to a full and satisfying life can they be significantly related to the rest of the general education program.

A second important factor in this problem is the need for assessing and evaluating all educational experiences in terms of their contributions to the life of the student. The purpose of all education is to improve the quality of the student's living, and in too many cases we have tended to think in terms of "essential subject matter" rather than desirable behavior. It is necessary, first of all, that there be some agreement as to what constitutes desirable behavior. The kinds of educational experiences which are provided will then be determined by the effectiveness with which they induce such behavior. The student himself—his understanding, his attitudes, and his behavior—provides the matrix, so to speak, within which educational experiences can be brought into meaningful relationships. Such orientation necessitates a kind of planning—an interchange and cross-fertilization between specialists in various subject-matter areas—which has been all too rare in education. It is only as the teachers who have direct responsibility for the educational experiences of their students are able to achieve a unified view of life and of education that these experiences will have the unity and relatedness which is so essential but so conspicuously lacking from much of contemporary college education.

The third major aspect of this problem has to do with suiting educational experiences to the life of the individual student for it is here that the final test must be made with respect to the relatedness and integration of any educational program. A blueprint for an education which is conceived in the abstract may exhibit a beautiful unity and relationship of parts, but its worth must be determined by its appropriateness to the human material for which it has been designed. Unless it has significance for the individual and is so designed as to develop his potentialities and meet his needs it cannot be called an integrated education. It is essential, therefore, that, through counseling and guidance, each student's program be planned as a unified whole in terms of his particular needs, interests, and abilities. The problem of relating instruction in the arts to the rest of the general education program is then a part of the total problem of providing an education which is related in all its parts.

INTEGRATING THE OFFERINGS IN THE VARIOUS ARTS

While there are certain esthetic principles which are common to all the arts, the interrelationships between them are frequently obscured by their more obvious and apparent differences. Often it is the specialists in one medium or another who, because of their greater attention to the problems peculiar to their particular medium, exhibit the least understanding of those forms of artistic expression which are outside their own narrow field. McGrath has pointed out that among college instructors in the various arts it is difficult to find individuals who have much understanding of any of the art mediums outside their own particular specialty. He comments that "It does seem a bit odd to expect a student to integrate facts and principles in various branches of a discipline when the members of the faculty are unwilling or incapable of doing so." [2] It seems clear, therefore, that if students are to integrate their understandings of the various mediums of the arts specific attention must be given to the problem, for such understanding cannot be counted on to develop by itself.

In the majority of instances, the arts—the visual arts, music, drama, literature, and the dance—are taught quite independently of each other and it remains for the student to integrate his learnings in the various courses into a unified pattern. This is true in the case of those students who are fortunate enough or interested enough to take course work in more than one art area. For those who, because of program limitations or for other reasons, have contact with only one area, there is but the minimum of opportunity to explore the relationships which it may bear to other mediums of the arts, for, while individual instructors may in their teaching make frequent reference to other art forms, there is no assurance that this will be the case.

Several reasons are generally offered for maintaining separate courses in the various arts. One of them has already been suggested: the narrowly specialized interest of many teachers which makes them more or less indifferent to fields of the arts not their own. Furthermore, the assumption underlying the entire free elective system of education that the individual student can, without assistance, integrate his learnings in many widely separated areas has been as influential in the teaching of the arts as in any other area. Another reason given for the superiority of this type of organization is that any course which attempts to synthesize several art areas must inevitably be superficial in its approach and that it is better for students to have a deep experience in one area than to have shallow experiences in several. Thus, Longman, in discussing courses which attempt to integrate the arts, has written:

. . . such a course includes too much. The instructor might give unity and coherence to such a wealth of material by making it a course in aesthetics with suitable illustrations from the arts, with

[2] *Ibid.,* p. 44.

bits of information about their history, and a generous indulgence in interesting generalizations. This is not what we require, however, for the student will not have time for significant experiences in any one of the arts. He will feel at home in none, but will learn to talk glibly about any. He may know an array of principles systematically, but will not understand them intuitively or apply them unconsciously.[3]

Another argument offered by Longman in favor of separate course organization is that, from the standpoint of teaching personnel, courses which attempt to integrate the arts are doomed to failure. He says:

Eclectic courses conducted by a succession of different specialists are clearly unsuited to our purposes as well as generally unsuccessful in any area. Nor is any single man competent to teach such a course at the college level, where the teacher must be a master of his subject. . . . We do not now and will not in the future expect the man who can paint to be able to dance, or the man who can design a building to be able to act or write a symphony. The fine arts have little in common beside the aesthetic component and a related history. Although the educative value of each is similar, the specialist in one does not categorically need to study any other, as, for example, the chemist needs mathematics and physics and the psychologist biology, or as the political scientist needs economics and sociology, and as the student of one foreign language must know others.[4]

This statement also indicates one further reason which is often given in support of limiting courses to one area of the arts: that the relationships between the arts are not nearly as significant as we often suppose them to be and that understanding in one area of the arts will contribute little, if anything, to a deeper appreciation and understanding in another area.

Some of these arguments would appear to be open to question and will be examined further in paragraphs which follow. It suffices at this point to note them as the reasons which are generally given for maintaining separate courses in each of the arts. One of the chief advantages of this type of organization is that it gives the individual instructor the greatest possible freedom and there is no danger of his being hampered by having to make

[3] In Earl J. McGrath and others, *Toward General Education* (New York: The Macmillan Company, 1948), p. 192.
[4] *Ibid.*, pp. 191–92.

concessions to points of view at variance with his own. Further-more, it offers him the maximum of security for he need not deal with any area save the one in which he is an authority, nor is his point of view in danger of being seriously challenged by authorities in other areas of the arts. This is obviously an advantage, for the insecure teacher is generally the ineffective one. A further point in favor of this type of organization is that, while it offers no assurance that students will have significant experiences in their one chosen field of art, it does not present the same obstacles to such experiences as are apt to be found in courses of a more inclusive nature. However, if we proceed from the assumption that there are significant and important relationships between the arts and that an understanding of these relationships can contribute to the student's esthetic development, it must be concluded that this type of organization yields the smallest dividends in terms of such understandings.

In a number of instances, where courses in the various arts are taught quite independently, a conscious attempt is made in each to emphasize common esthetic features and to give particular attention to the interrelationships between the arts. At least in terms of stated objectives, this has the definite advantage that the problem is recognized and there is a conscious attempt to deal with it. However, there is little about this system to insure that the interrelationships between the arts will, in fact, be adequately dealt with. While it is true that no organization will itself provide assurance of successful, or even adequate, teaching, some kinds of organization do have greater potentialities than others for the realization of specific ends. In this particular case, the integration of the arts would appear to be left almost entirely to the discretion of the individual instructor. Its success, therefore, would depend, to a large extent, upon the importance which each instructor attaches to the problem of relating his field to the other arts. Furthermore, unless specific provision is made for interdepartmental planning, differences among instructors in approach to their subjects, in vocabulary, in manner of presenting their material—in all the factors which go into teaching—might be so great as to render their most sincere efforts in this direction more confusing than illuminating to their students.

Basilius, in describing an integrated program in the arts at Wayne University,[5] has commented particularly on the problems faced by a group of specialists from the various arts in trying to arrive at common understandings and a common vocabulary. Unless specific attention is given to this problem by means of interdepartmental planning, the efforts of individual instructors to relate their courses to the experiences which students have had or are having in other courses could at best, it seems, be only partially successful.

The point of view taken here is that this is a problem which warrants serious attention and that it can be adequately met only if it is treated as a problem of central, and not merely incidental, concern. In answer to the statement that the arts "have little in common beside the esthetic component and a related history" it may be asked whether this is not a great deal to have in common and whether it does not provide an adequate basis for the development of meaningful and illuminating relationships. The common esthetic elements to be found in all the arts are, first, a pre-eminent concern with the life of emotion and feeling—the expressive element—and, second, a concern with organization and with relationships—the formal element.

To state that these two elements provide the basis for an integrated treatment of the arts frequently brings cries of protest because, it is stated, with respect to the expressive element, each of the arts has its particular métier and deals with different aspects of the sentient and emotional life; in the same way, though each of the arts has a formal element, concepts of form vary greatly from one medium to another in accordance with the properties of the particular medium. It is precisely because of these differences, however, that a comparative study of the arts is so important and can contribute so much to esthetic perception. If the expressive and the formal qualities of all the arts were identical, then, indeed, there would be less reason for an integrated treatment of them for we could expect that there might be some transfer of learning from one medium to another. The fact that each medium does have distinctive qualities means

[5] H. A. Basilius, "An Open Letter Addressed to the Dean of an Arts College," *Journal of Higher Education*, XVI (November, 1945), 427.

that it can be better understood and appreciated if it is studied in comparison with other mediums.

In the teaching of the visual arts, there is generally some emphasis placed on the differences between the various mediums —their potentialities and their limitations. The medium of fresco is peculiarly suited to certain types of expression and, by virtue of its physical properties, imposes particular limitations of form while at the same time it offers unique possibilities for formal organization. By comparison, the mediums of etching, watercolor, wood sculpture, and oil painting each have properties which make them peculiarly suited to other kinds of expression and formal organization. Through a comparison of these various mediums the special characteristics and potentialities of each can be more fully understood and appreciated. In the same way, a comparison of musical expression with graphic expression, of dance forms with literary forms, of any of these with the dramatic medium, by highlighting the unique characteristics of each of them can heighten and sharpen the understanding and appreciation of them all. From the standpoint of content, therefore, there seems to be little more reason for maintaining these major divisions in the arts than there would be for keeping oil painting separate from sculpture, or industrial design separate from etching.

In spite of the difficulties which it may present, the approach which seems best adapted to integrating the arts and providing the student with the "esthetic education" of which Mursell speaks would be a single course dealing with all the arts but, at the same time, allowing the student to give special attention to an area of his own choosing. Such a course would have a dual organization, being divided between general sessions attended by all the students and small laboratory groups in each of the art areas. The core sessions would be taught by a panel of instructors, one from each of the art areas. This part of the course would include lecture-discussion activities, actual performances or presentations in various art forms, and field trips. Each student would be free to choose the laboratory section of greatest interest to him, and the emphasis, here, of course, would be on creative activity and actual experience with the art medium.

In a number of such courses, as for example at Wayne University, the attempt has been made to have every student participate actively in each of the art forms. Thus, during that part of the course devoted to poetry, all the students do creative writing, and when the lecture-discussion sessions turn to the visual arts, they all do work in the art studio. This procedure does not seem to make adequate provision for the great differences between students in interests and capabilities. It cannot be assumed, for example, that an experience in creative writing will be equally meaningful to all students. An individual with a predominantly verbal intelligence who thinks and feels in terms of verbal images may find this a most rewarding experience; but for another person who is more sensitive to visual imagery and less able to express his feelings verbally such an experience may offer little, and he may be quite incapable of satisfactory—that is to say, satisfying—achievement in this medium. There may be other individuals who will be unable to achieve satisfactory results in visual mediums, or in music, or in the dance. In order, therefore, that the creative experiences of each student should have the maximum significance for him, it would seem advisable that he should be allowed to select the area or areas in which he feels the greatest interest and from which he will derive the greatest satisfaction.

Furthermore, in these laboratory activities, it is important not only that the student should be working in a medium which is congenial and from which he can derive a sense of accomplishment and satisfaction but also that he should experience the medium with depth and intensity. The conditions necessary to achieve such intensity will vary considerably with the individual, particularly with respect to the matter of time. For the majority of students, new and unaccustomed to creative activity in the arts, it will not come easily within the matter of a few weeks. Such students should be encouraged to continue in a single area of laboratory activity until they have attained the fullest measure of understanding which is possible in terms of their individual potentialities. Other students, who have a more extensive background in the arts or a greater capacity for creative activity, may be able to move more rapidly from one type of laboratory experience to another. Since the basic criterion for the students' creative activities is depth rather than variety, the number of areas in which any individual will actively participate must be decided in terms of his particular capacities and needs.

In a course such as this there may be many opportunities for students to have some contact with laboratory activities outside the area in which they are working, even though they may not participate directly. Such contacts could be made possible through the development of collaborative projects among the various studio groups. Projects may be centered in such activities as dance or drama presentations, the preparation of publications and exhibits, or the production of short experimental films, to mention but a few possibilities. Thus, while the students in the dance studio are composing and rehearsing simple compositions for presentation, the members of the visual arts group may design and produce costumes and scenic backgrounds; or patterns in rhythm which have been developed by members of the music group may be used by the dance students as accompaniments for their compositions. By means of such collaborative projects, each student may have contact with creative work which is being done in areas other than his own while, at the same time, he continues to concentrate on the field of his particular interest.

This type of course would appear to solve the problem of varied experiences versus deep experiences by providing the opportunity for both. The core sessions would be devoted to a comprehensive treatment which would deal with all the major areas of the arts. At the same time the laboratory sessions would give the student the opportunity for deeper exploration and experience in one particular area while, through such collaborative projects as might be developed, he would have contact with creative work being done in other areas.

In spite of the organization of the course, there is the possibility that the core sessions may degenerate into nothing more than a series of independent and unrelated segments as each instructor takes over for his brief period. Likewise, in courses of this type, it sometimes happens that little conscious effort is made to relate laboratory activities to the work of the core session and any relationships which may exist are purely fortuitous. Both of these dangers can be avoided, however, by careful staff planning. The most important aspect of the problem is the necessity for all the staff members, within certain broad limits, to have a common viewpoint with respect to both the purposes and the procedures of the course. It hardly seems necessary or even desirable that all the instructors should have identical points of view. Difference and disagreement, so long as they stay within the matrix of a larger background, may often serve to give the student a broader understanding of the arts than will a series of thoroughly consistent viewpoints. But very sharp differences in concepts, in methods, even in vocabulary, may be most disruptive in their effects.

Critics of this type of course frequently support their criticism with the statement that it is impossible for a group of specialists from various fields of the arts to arrive at the necessary meeting of minds. That it is difficult to achieve can certainly not be denied. On the other hand, teaching itself should be an educative experience and we can reasonably expect that instructors will have, to some degree at least, the adaptability, the flexibility, and the capacity to meet new situations constructively, which they demand of their students. If they are convinced of the importance and the validity of an integrated approach to the arts, and are willing to subject themselves to an uncomfortable uprooting of their prejudices, it should be possible, though not easy, to reach the common ground which is essential for the successful operation of a course of this kind.

One further problem remains to be discussed with respect to this type of course. This has to do with the various ways in which the subject-matter content may be selected and organized to the end that each of the arts individually will be most adequately dealt with while at the same time their relationships will be most fully explored and understood. Since this problem must be met in any course, regardless of organization or the specific art forms being dealt with, it will be treated as a separate topic in the succeeding section and, where appropriate, specific reference will be made to the type of course which has been described here.

SELECTION AND ORGANIZATION OF
COURSE CONTENT

SOME CONSIDERATIONS RELATIVE TO THE PROBLEMS
OF SELECTION AND ORGANIZATION

Decisions with respect to the selection and organization of subject matter are based primarily on two factors: the purpose which a course is set up to achieve, and the nature of human learning. Growing out of these factors are a number of considerations which have particular relevance to instruction in the arts.

The first point to be mentioned is that experience in the arts has certain unique values for human living. The basis of this uniqueness has already been discussed and it is necessary here only to point out the importance of this concept for the selection and organization of course content. Much college art instruction has suffered from the attempt to make it as nearly as possible like instruction in other disciplines and the essential characteristics of the art experience have been largely neglected. The most worth-while values of art experience—which are also the unique ones—can be fully realized only if they provide the central motivation for art instruction.

In Chapter II mention was made of the importance of student needs and interests in the learning process. For at least two reasons this concept has especial significance in the area of the arts. In the first place, as compared with the sciences or the so-called tool subjects, the arts are relatively new and unfamiliar territory for the great majority of students. In some cases, in fact, art has been confused with the "arty" and has been met with resistance. For this reason it is considerably more difficult for students to relate the arts to their own particular needs and interests than is the case with subject matter areas which are more familiar to them. Also, because of the great emphasis in our culture on practical values it is exceedingly difficult for many students to see the relevance of the arts to their own lives. Because of these facts, the problem of relating art instruction to the felt needs and interests of students is a crucial one, and this principle of human learning takes on particular significance in the selection and organization of course content.

The second reason for the importance of this concept in art instruction is to be found in the fact that art experience, properly understood, is essentially creative in character. We have seen that creative activity is the process by which the individual reintegrates and reconstructs his own experiences—his understandings and his emotional and intuitive reactions—into new patterns. Such activity cannot be forced into patterns which are foreign to the individual's concepts and values for as soon as this happens the activity ceases to be creative. The student's own needs and interests, therefore, are the only possible basis for meaningful experiences in the arts.

Closely related to the foregoing point is the importance of building on the individual's present knowledges and understandings. Even if we assume that students approaching the relatively unfamiliar territory of the arts may exhibit an intense interest and enthusiasm, we cannot expect that they will be responsive to, or will be able fully to comprehend, concepts or experiences which have only an obscure relation to their present fund of knowledge and understanding. The road from boogie-woogie to Schoenberg, or from the comic strip to the Chinese scroll painting, is a long one for most people and must usually be traveled by a process of gradually enlarged insights and understandings. We would scarcely expect students in a beginning class in physics to grasp the full meaning and significance of Einstein's theory of relativity, nor would we think of giving beginners in mathematics problems in calculus. While it is true that such analogies between the arts and the sciences are dangerous and cannot be pushed too far, it does seem that in art instruction we should give more attention to where the students are when they come to us and what they are capable of integrating into their present fund of knowledge and understanding. In the course of their college art experiences some students may not travel as far as we might hope on the road of esthetic perception and understanding, but it does seem better to give them a sure footing and a continuing movement forward than to overwhelm them at the very start and thus discourage them from ever making a beginning.

In Chapter VIII, some attention was given to the importance of emphasizing the contemporary arts as well as the reasons for such emphasis. Hughes Mearns has commented as follows regarding the importance of understanding contemporary artistic expression:

Our experience would tell us that the best route to that true spirit of reverence for the past is first to accumulate appreciative power through exercise in the more approachable love for the work of living artists. . . .

. . . . . .

To miss these . . . phenomena is to have been alive in 1600 and not to have heard of Shakespeare, to be another Zio Battista di Tommaso, who never once looked up to the works of his fellow townsman, Michelangelo. Future historians will be writing of this our wealth; it is a squandering of more than fortune to be untouched by its vitalizing influence.[6]

Giving greater attention to contemporary arts need not necessarily mean neglecting the arts of the past. It is essential, however, that we recognize the significance which the contemporary arts can and should have in the lives of students and revise our teaching accordingly. As Barr has said, ". . . the cogent importance of twentieth century art lies not so much in the greatness of its achievement as in this one simple, obvious, and overwhelming fact—the twentieth century happens to be the period in which we are living. It is our century: we have made it and we've got to study it, understand it, get some joy out of it, *master* it." [7] So long as art instruction continues to emphasize the historic arts at the expense of contemporary expression, the full meaning and significance of the arts of today cannot be realized.

Because art instruction in general education is primarily concerned with developing esthetic awareness and sensitivity to the individual's total environment, the content of such instruction

[6] Hughes Mearns, *The Creative Adult* (New York: Doubleday & Company, Inc., 1940), pp. 179, 181–82.
[7] Alfred H. Barr, "Modern Art Makes History Too," *College Art Journal*, I (November, 1941), 3.

must extend beyond the limits of the so-called fine arts to include all the plastic and graphic arts—the arts of daily life as well as the arts of the museum and the studio. These more common artistic expressions are the ones with which the average layman is most intimately concerned in his daily living and are the sources of the most constant, even though not the deepest, satisfactions. While great works of contemporary and historic art may unquestionably be the richest sources of esthetic experience, still, to neglect the more common arts of everyday living is to present a distorted picture, to rob the individual of many rich sources of human satisfaction, and to perpetuate the already common fallacy of art as something apart from the processes of daily living.

POSSIBLE BASES FOR THE SELECTION AND ORGANIZATION
OF CONTENT

Against the background of the above comments and the earlier discussion of the purpose of instruction in the arts, it is now possible to examine the various ways in which the subject matter of the arts may be approached. The following paragraphs will be devoted to a discussion of a number of emphases which have been found to characterize instruction in the arts. Save in a few cases, these emphases are rarely found to constitute the sole approach to the arts in any given course; but, by and large, one or another of them will be found to predominate and to exert a basic influence with respect to the kind of subject matter that is dealt with and the manner in which it is handled. In the discussion which follows, the attempt will be made to evaluate each emphasis or approach in terms of the purpose of the art program in general education and the kinds of instructional procedures that seem best adapted to a realization of such purposes.

The most common emphasis in courses designed for the general student is on the chronological development of the arts. The historical survey, especially in the visual arts, attempts to cover the entire course of Western civilization, with sometimes brief excursions into the arts of the Orient and pre-Columbian America, and the finest examples of the arts in each period are studied. In varying degrees, attention is given to the distinctively esthetic problems involved in the study of the arts and to the broad cultural context out of which they have grown. Historical development frequently provides the unifying principle for an integrated approach to the arts, in which case all the major art forms of a culture epoch are studied simultaneously.

So long as the historical approach concentrates on the larger aspects of esthetic and cultural development, it can be of considerable value in helping the student to gain a broader perspective on his own life and times and a better understanding and appreciation of the arts of today. While it is generally the avowed purpose of art history courses to develop such understandings as will have significance for a fuller appreciation of the arts and a deeper insight into contemporary living, it happens in all too many cases that the delights of historical study for its own sake dissuade the instructor from this purpose. The student who does not have the historian's special interest and point of view is left with nothing but a collection of names and dates, and poorly remembered images from a slide projector. The chief emphasis tends to be on chronological development rather than on the esthetic experience itself and the student emerges from the course with little real understanding or appreciation. With respect to this aspect of the historical approach, Ducasse has made the following comments:

The truth about college art courses in the history and analysis of the various arts is, I believe, that opportunity for cultivating aesthetic appreciation is provided by these courses only incidentally, through the fact that they acquaint the students with a wide variety of works of the particular art they are concerned with. But even this opportunity is interfered with by the fact that in these courses what the student is called upon to do is to learn, memorize, think, analyze; and this is a sort of activity radically different from the prolonged, quiet contemplation from which alone results the aesthetic response proper. These courses habituate those who take them to the former approach and by so doing automatically tend to dishabituate them from the latter.[8]

Another objection to such courses is that they deal almost exclusively with the fine arts and neglect all those areas of art

[8] C. S. Ducasse, "Art Appreciation and the Curriculum," *Association of American Colleges Bulletin*, XXVII (October, 1941), 431–32.

which, as we have seen, lie much closer to the life of the average person. Furthermore, because they deal only with the great masterpieces of art, students, in many cases, have no contact whatever with original works in the visual arts. It seems completely fallacious to assume that, having seen a black-and-white photograph of Chartres Cathedral, the student has experienced this building in its full significance, or that a colored slide projection of a Giotto fresco can communicate the same message that the original does. While it may be extremely important that the student should have some indirect experience with these masterpieces of art, it is equally important that he should have a wealth of direct experiences, even though these may have to be with products of a somewhat inferior nature.

Mention has already been made of the tendency, in historical courses, to slight the contemporary arts. The following statement is typical of the attitude of a disturbingly large number of art historians:

Art itself is largely a recovery of the memory of the ages from threatened oblivion, and the short and confused memory of the present is not sufficiently consolidated to be a major subject of study. . . .

. . . I by no means regard the modern field as barred to the student. For many years I endeavored to teach modern painting up to what was then yesterday. In devoting only two or three lectures to twentieth century painting I hoped I was giving it its relative importance in the splended succession from Rubens and Caravaggio to Renoir and Eakins.[9]

This statement, while it is certainly not typical of all teachers who use the historical approach, does illustrate a tendency which many of them exhibit, because their gaze is fixed in the past, to regard the contemporary arts as being of relatively little importance as compared with the total span of man's cultural achievements. This point of view completely disregards the idea that, for the person living today, the arts of his own time, simply because they *are* of his own time, have the greatest significance. Combined with this is the natural tendency, in any course, to linger too long at the beginning and to move too fast at the end.

[9] Frank Jewett Mather, "Old Art or New," *College Art Journal*, I (January, 1942), 31.

These two factors together conspire to give the student only the most cursory glance at the art which is of his own life and time.

A final objection to the historical emphasis is that it does not lend itself to integration with studio activities. In some instances the attempt is made to relate activities in the laboratory to historical studies by having members of the class do studio work in the manner of the period being studied. Thus, during that part of the course devoted to Egyptian art, they paint in the style of the Egyptians, and when attention is turned to the Baroque period, they produce examples of Baroque art. If the purpose of studio work is to provide opportunity for creative activity, this is obviously a most unsatisfactory procedure. Its only possible value is that it may shed some light on the formal characteristics of historic arts and on the technical procedures which were used by artists of the past; it can certainly do little to help the student give expression to his own esthetic impulses and perceptions.

Another emphasis approaches the arts from the standpoint of their social background and the cultural context out of which they have developed. While the various culture epochs are generally dealt with in historic sequence, the emphasis is not so much on mere chronology but rather on the arts as they reflect the ideas, values, and cultural patterns which have characterized the great epochs in the history of the world. The primary advantage of this approach is that it does provide a broad and comprehensive view of the arts and enables the student to see them in their manifold relationships to other aspects of cultural development. By seeing how the arts have functioned in cultures other than his own, he may gain a better understanding of their role, both actual and potential, in contemporary culture. When used as a method for integrating the arts, it provides a more comprehensive view of a cultural period than is possible in the treatment of any single art form. In studying the Renaissance, for example, an understanding of the music, the literature, the architecture, painting and sculpture of that period will provide a fuller and more comprehensive view of the period than will a study of any one of these arts by itself. Furthermore, comparison of the various art forms as expressions of the same or similar ideas and values may serve to clarify the student's understanding of the distinctive qualities and characteristics of each of the art forms. Probably the greatest danger of this emphasis, when it is used to the exclusion of others, is that it will become a study of cultural ideas rather than a study of art and that the arts themselves will assume a role of secondary importance as mere illustrations of the central motif. To use Northrop's terminology, the arts will be considered only in terms of their second function (see pp. 73-74) and their distinctively esthetic qualities will be slighted. This may be entirely appropriate in certain humanities courses where the main stress is on the development of cultural ideals, but it provides only a partial solution for courses in which the arts themselves are the primary focus.

This emphasis, furthermore, presents some of the same difficulties as the purely historical approach. Common to both is the assumption that the surest way to develop esthetic sensitivity is to expose the uninitiated student immediately to the great historic masterpieces of art. Such thinking fails to consider whether the student with a limited background and understanding is ready for, or receptive to, these masterpieces. An eventual appreciation of them may be better assured, and even accelerated, by beginning with situations which are more familiar to the student and more definitely within his range of understanding. Furthermore, such an emphasis, concentrating as it does on great masterpieces of art, will probably offer little opportunity for meaningful integration with studio activities. With particular respect to the visual arts, there is one further difficulty which this approach has in common with the historical approach: that there is little, if any, direct contact with original works of art. While this may not be entirely true in large urban centers where museum collections are available, it presents a very real problem where there are no such facilities to draw upon.

Another emphasis, which is characteristic of courses dealing more specifically with the development of appreciation, deals with the formal principles of artistic expression. In the visual arts, stress is placed on such principles as balance, dominance, rhythm, unity and variety, and on the various plastic elements as they contribute to the formal organization of the art object. Appropriate works of art are used as illustrations of these principles. When used as the basis for an integrated approach to the arts, the principles must, of necessity, be somewhat modified and broadened, but the method is essentially the same. Thus, in describing "The Humanities," a course offered at the University of Florida, Shoemaker states that it "opens with a survey of aesthetic principles common to all the arts—dominance, unity, repetition—and in literature, specialized considerations of diction and imagery." [10]

This kind of organization has several advantages over the two preceding ones. In the first place, it need not deal so exclusively with the arts of the past as the others are apt to do; also, it need not be limited to a consideration of the fine arts. The formal principles of plastic organization can be as effectively demonstrated with a ten-cent-store coffee cup or a Charles Eames chair as with the Parthenon or the "David" of Michelangelo; in music, certain aspects of rhythmic structure can perhaps be better illustrated with a recent jazz recording than with examples from the classic masterpieces. The range of material which may be drawn upon is thus greatly widened and there is the possibility, through using examples with which the students have some familiarity, of relating instruction more closely to their present backgrounds and interests. A still further advantage of this method is that it offers a much better basis for relating lecture-discussion activities to studio experiences.

The great weakness of such an emphasis is that the activities in both the classroom and the studio, while they may be closely related, will be of a highly formalistic nature, for the total concern is with what may be called the grammar of art. One does not perceive the emotional significance of a sonnet by scanning it, nor will one be moved to an expression of his innermost feelings if he is given a laboratory problem dealing with the principle of balance. With particular respect to an integrated program, so long as formal principles provide the dominant emphasis it would seem impossible to maintain a close relation-

[10] Francis Shoemaker, *Aesthetic Experience and the Humanities* (New York: Columbia University Press, 1943), p. 160.

ship between lecture-discussion and laboratory activities and at the same time develop the kind of collaborative projects described earlier. For such projects do not grow out of a systematic development of the formal principles of artistic composition. They spring out of the interests and desires of the students; they are idea-centered and not method-centered. This statement, in fact, summarizes the great shortcoming of this approach, for it side-steps almost completely the emotional and expressive aspects of the arts which are their motivation and their essence. Such understanding and appreciation as the students do attain, therefore, is apt to be cold and formalistic and concerned almost entirely with the means by which expression has been achieved without reference to the expression itself.

Because every artistic object is conceived in terms of some medium or material and involves the use of certain technical procedures, this provides another method through which understanding of the arts may be approached. In the visual arts, this emphasis has probably received its fullest development at the Bauhaus, and subsequently at the School of Design in Chicago. It has attracted many adherents and has had a widespread influence. Primary emphasis is placed on the physical properties of the materials of art and the potentialities which each material, in consequence of its physical properties, has for plastic organization. A typical laboratory problem employing this approach would be the construction of a "texture scale" in which are combined a series of materials such as wood, sandpaper, metal shavings, leather, and cloth in accordance with their particular tactile qualities. Or the student may take a single material and, through experimentation, discover all the possible ways in which it may be manipulated. Through such exploration, he discovers the unique properties of materials and their potentialities for plastic organization and expression.

A related method may be used in an integrated approach to the arts by considering the medium or mediums of each of the major art forms and the influence which their unique properties exert on problems of expression and organization. For example, the dance, because it uses the movement of the human body as its medium, is adapted to certain kinds of organization and expression which may be impossible to achieve in musical or dramatic form, or can be achieved only through a gross distortion of them. A specific example may be seen in the changes which must be made in adapting a novel to dramatic or cinematic form. Because of the difference in medium, the entire formal structure must be altered and, equally important, the resulting emotional and esthetic impact is not the same.

The value of this approach in developing an understanding of the arts may be considerable, for by emphasizing the unique properties of the various artistic mediums it can give fuller meaning to generalized concepts of expression and formal organization. Furthermore, by directing attention to the materials themselves it may develop in the student a fuller sensuous awareness and a delight in the experiencing of materials for their own sake. Because it proceeds from a consideration of actual physical and sensory phenomena, the possibilities for illustrative material and for laboratory activities are extensive, and the experiences in both classroom and studio can be closely related to the student's background of understanding and knowledge. At the same time, there is the danger that this approach, through too great a concentration on materials and methods for their own sake, will lead to an exclusive concern with the technical aspects of artistic production at the expense of the expressive function of the arts and their unique relevance to the inner life of the individual and the social context out of which they develop.

An emphasis which is better suited to the visual arts alone than to an integrated program concentrates on the role of art in the daily life of the individual. Here, stress is placed on the potential art experiences which are a part of the student's day-to-day activities, such as the selection of clothes and motorcars, of household furnishings and utensils, and on the development of good taste with respect to the many objects of art in the student's environment. Probably the greatest advantage of this approach is that it relates itself closely to the needs and interests of students by focusing attention on art experiences which are a part of the common life of the times. Not only does it deal with material which is within the understanding and experience of the students; it also has the advantage of being able to deal directly with actual objects in the student's environment, rather than having to rely largely on reproductions, and it centers its attention on the arts of the contemporary world.

There are, however, several weaknesses which, though not necessarily inherent in this approach, are often found to accompany it. In the first place, it tends to be limited to the development of "good taste," to a rather superficial ability to discriminate between well-designed and poorly designed objects without any very basic understanding of the esthetic experience itself. There is also the tendency to overemphasize the consumer aspects of daily living and to neglect the student's need for a more direct kind of expression in the materials of art. The line of reasoning appears to be that since most people, in their daily activities, do not engage in creative arts, there is little reason to develop their capacity for creative activity. By the same token, there is the tendency to neglect the fine arts with the idea that since most people have very little contact with them today they are of secondary importance to the average student. The difficulties which have been enumerated here are not basic to this approach but rather grow out of a too narrow concept of the role of the arts in our daily living.

Closely related to the foregoing, but proceeding from somewhat more basic concepts, is the approach which deals with the visual arts as the solution of human problems. The focus here is broadened from the rather narrower concerns with the daily activities of living to include the relevance of the esthetic factor to the entire range of human activities. The arts are generally related, in this approach, to major areas of living such as the home, the community, religion, commerce, industry, and recreation. Each area is dealt with as it presents unique possibilities for esthetic expression and experience.

As with the art in daily living approach, this one has the advantage that it proceeds from a concept of life activities which is familiar to the student. It is grounded in the life which students live today and the relevance of art experience to that life. At the same time, it is not nearly so apt to be limited to a narrow concern with the development of good taste and the ability to discriminate between "good" art and "poor" art; because of its more basic concepts and its broader focus on the problems of human living, as compared with the more restricted emphasis on the day-to-day activities of the student, it has the potentialities for dealing with the arts in a more fundamental way as the expression of significant human values in the various areas of living. Moreover, because it does not limit itself to the great masterpieces of art, which are generally inaccessible save in small reproductions or slides, it offers the possibility of direct contact with a variety of art products. With respect to studio activities, it offers manifold opportunities for a close relationship between the more formal instruction of the lecture-discussion period and creative work in art mediums.

With respect to both classroom and studio activities, however, this approach presents one rather serious problem arising from the fact that it is organized in terms of areas of living as indicated above. So long as the arts are treated solely in relation to specific areas of living such as the home, the community, or industry, there is a tendency to deal with them only in their utilitarian aspects. Art is studied as a solution to the problem of providing shelter, of building cities, or selling and producing goods, and the expressive quality of the art object is relegated to second place. In dealing with the arts which are primarily utilitarian this approach is entirely satisfactory; but the problem becomes difficult when it comes to dealing with those arts which do not have a utilitarian basis—specifically, the fine arts. The paintings of Picasso and Braque, or the sculpture of Brancusi, cannot easily be related to any specific area of living except the esthetic area, for these are esthetic experiences which are not related in any obvious way to the pursuits of our daily living; nor can they be called the solution to any problem except the problem of expressing the sentient and emotional life. In the same way, the student in the studio who is expressing his most private and ineffable feelings in paint cannot be said to be working on the solution of a problem in any of the areas which this organization includes.

For this same reason, an approach of this kind is not well adapted to an integrated treatment of the arts, for in the other art fields—music, the literary forms, and the dance—the relationship between expression and the specific areas of living becomes even more obscure. The symphonies of Beethoven, for example, or the novels of Hemingway, cannot be dealt with in these dimensions. They must be dealt with, first and foremost, as the solution to problems of human expression above and beyond any specific areas of living.

It is, of course, of the utmost importance that the student be able to see the arts in relation to his daily living—that he should understand their significance for him as a member of a family, as a worker, as a member of a community group. The preceding statements are by no means meant to imply that the arts are to be treated as something precious and esoteric, and out of the reach of our daily living. What they do imply, however, is that the basic referent should be broad enough to allow for adequate treatment of all the manifestations of the esthetic impulse.

Such a referent is the expressive quality which is the basis of all works of art and this, it would seem, is the unifying principle around which instruction in the arts can be most advantageously organized. Only as this aspect of the arts is given pre-eminence will the distinctive and essential quality of esthetic experience be seen in its full import. Furthermore, with this as the focus—the controlling idea—the other emphases which have been enumerated here fall into position.

Each of the approaches to an understanding of the arts which has been discussed in the foregoing paragraphs has been shown to have certain values, for each approaches the arts from a different direction, cuts through them, so to speak, in a different dimension. But no one of them is adequate by itself because each illuminates only a segment—sometimes larger, sometimes smaller —of the esthetic totality. What is needed, therefore, is a unifying idea, a basic referent, which will bring all these varying emphases into a coherent relationship.

Because expression is the essential source of all artistic creation, and the end as well, it is toward an understanding of the arts as expression that a course of the kind being considered here should be directed. At the same time, merely to say that the expressive quality of the arts should be the central emphasis has little meaning, for it is rather like saying that there shall be spirit without body, or end without means. The fact is, however, that artistic expression is, first of all, expression of an individual's response to his environment; it is always related to a background of cultural ideas; it is conceived in terms of some medium, whether this be stone, paint, words, tones, or movement; the material is given a form in which may be perceived certain principles of organization; and the resulting expressive object has relevance to some aspect of the life we live today. Each of these facts represents a different facet of the expressive act or the expressive object and all are necessary for a complete understanding of it.

It appears, therefore, that each of the approaches or emphases which have been considered can make the fullest contribution to an understanding of the arts when it is seen in its particular relationship to the unifying principle of expression.[11] As each is considered in its relation to this basic idea, its particular relevance to the esthetic whole will be revealed, and rather than being an end in itself it will be one of several means for a fuller understanding of that essential factor from which esthetic experience derives its unique quality.

PROPOSED ORGANIZATION FOR AN INTEGRATED
APPROACH TO THE ARTS

In the light of the foregoing discussion it is now possible to indicate the general outlines of an integrated course which employs the expressive aspect of the arts as its unifying principle. Before proceeding, however, one point should be clarified with respect to this discussion. While this entire study is concerned chiefly with the visual arts, it proceeds from a point of view which holds that there are certain concepts basic to all the major forms of artistic expression. It holds, furthermore, that the needs of the general student will be best served not by limiting him to experience in one area of the arts, but by giving him contact with as many areas as possible in order that he may develop an

[11] The one emphasis which is not provided for in the above analysis is the historical approach. It was indicated earlier, however, that a knowledge of mere chronology is of little value in realizing the purposes of a course such as the one being considered here and that the historical course makes its most valuable contributions as it lends itself to other emphases.

understanding of those basic concepts which serve to unify them. In this way, it is believed, his understanding and appreciation of any one of the arts will be most effectively extended and deepened.

At the same time, it is recognized that, because of the various limitations existing in many situations with respect to staff and facilities, the kind of integrated program recommended here cannot be fully realized and, in many cases, a course combining all the arts may not be administratively feasible. However, the organization to be proposed in the following paragraphs is grounded in certain concepts which are believed to be basic to all the arts. It is suggested, therefore, that it is an approach which not only is applicable to an integrated program, but with certain modifications in accordance with the special characteristics of the various art forms, provides a basic approach to any of them. Likewise, it may be used in courses combining only two or three of the major art forms, for its successful operation does not depend upon the inclusion of all the arts.

It should be reiterated that the present study is motivated primarily by an interest in the visual arts and proceeds from a more extended knowledge and understanding in that area. However, the kind of integrated approach recommended here must result inevitably from the aforementioned convictions regarding the interrelatedness of the arts. It is to be hoped, therefore, that the inclusion of all the arts in this discussion will not be regarded as a presumptuous excursion into foreign fields, but rather as a necessary result of the point of view which is basic to the entire study.

It is in no way suggested that the organization to be proposed is the only way of achieving the purposes of an arts course in general education; but in terms of the point of view presented, it would appear to contribute most directly to the realization of desired outcomes. The structure of the course will be indicated primarily in terms of the lecture-discussion sessions since this is the part of the course which would be the common experience of all the students. Moreover, while the closest possible relationship is to be maintained between lecture-discussion and studio activities, it is desirable that the latter should remain relatively unstructured in order to provide the maximum opportunity for the pursuit of individual interests and student planning of activities.

The basic idea of the course, as has already been suggested, would be to explore the arts as vehicles for expressing the emotionally significant aspects of our life and our environment. This would be achieved by first focusing directly on the expressive aspect of the arts and then examining in turn the relationship which artistic expression bears to the cultural background, to the mediums of the arts, and to the formal principles of organization; finally, specific attention would be given to the role of the arts in our contemporary culture.

Accordingly, the first part of the course would explore, at the level of student understanding, the concept of the arts as the expression of emotionally significant relationships and the basic difference between esthetic perception and practical knowledge. In this part of the course especially it would be of crucial importance to relate the material under discussion as closely as possible to the student's fund of experience and understanding, for the concepts and attitudes which he develops with respect to this basic idea will establish a framework for all his subsequent experiences in the course. The starting point for such a discussion might well be the students' own concepts of esthetic experience. What is it? How does it differ from other kinds of experience? What is its meaning? What does it have to contribute to the life of the average person? From such a preliminary discussion, growing out of the students' own experiences, would develop a number of questions which would provide the basis for further exploration and discussion.

The illustrative material used in this part of the course should include examples drawn from all the arts, if possible. Here again, it is of especial importance that such illustrations as are used should proceed from the familiar to the unfamiliar in terms of the students' prior backgrounds. In demonstrating the expressive qualities of music, for example, rather than comparing a Bach fugue with Strauss's "Death and Transfiguration," it might be better to compare an example of Dixieland jazz with Ellington's "Mood Indigo." The student, having grasped some of the essential differences between these two examples (and, incidentally, having seen that they are not scorned by the instructor), might then be in a better position to perceive corresponding differences in compositions which, though more profound, are less familiar to him.

As the first part of the course is devoted to the arts as an expression of the individual's emotional life, the second major division would turn to a consideration of the relation of artistic expression to the total cultural pattern. While this problem could be handled in a number of ways, the one suggested here as probably the most rewarding would be a comparative approach in which the place of the arts in contemporary American culture would be contrasted with their role in one of the historic culture epochs as, for example, the Medieval period or the Renaissance. In many courses which deal with the arts in relation to cultural backgrounds, the method is first to examine the ideas and values of a culture period and then to discover the ways in which these ideas and values have been expressed in the arts. The method suggested here would use somewhat the opposite procedure and may be best described by using a specific example. With reference to painting, the attempt would be made to find answers to questions such as the following: How does the art of painting function in contemporary life as compared with the life of Medieval Europe? How is it related to the social structure? To the life of the individual? What are the primary concerns of the painter in contemporary society and what were they in Medieval society? What values does each express and what means does he use to express them? Within the framework of each society how do individual differences of artists color and affect their responses to cultural pressures?

By approaching the problem of the cultural background of the arts in this way emphasis will be placed on the arts as expressions of the culture rather than on the culture as it is expressed through the arts. Although primary emphasis would be on one particular culture epoch as compared with contemporary society, examples from other periods could be freely drawn upon to illuminate particular points and to provide a wider background of understanding. It should also be noted that such a direct focus on the arts themselves will make it easier to study and clarify the interaction between the individual artist, with his unique set of values and his own personal vision, and the cultural factors which condition his view of the world and his manner of expression. Another important aspect of the total problem would be a consideration of the decline of certain art forms and the emergence of others as a result of cultural factors. Most obvious examples are the decline of the illuminated manuscript with the invention of printing, and the development of the motion picture as a new art form characteristic of modern technological culture.

The third major emphasis of the course would deal with the various mediums of the arts and their potentialities for expression. It would deal with such questions as the following: What are the distinctive characteristics of each of the mediums of the arts? How do they differ and what are their similarities? How does each medium lend itself to expressive use and what are its unique expressive qualities? What are its limitations? How can we know whether a medium is being well used or is being forced to do things for which it is not suited?

Because the approach as suggested here does not differ in any essential respect from the description which has been given earlier (pp. 175–176), there is no need to discuss it further at this point. It is only necessary to reiterate that here, as in the rest of the course, the underlying principle which gives relevance to the exploration of this problem is the expressive quality of the arts. Each medium is studied, evaluated, and understood as it contributes to the solution of this basic problem.

It is likewise unnecessary to discuss at any length the next major emphasis of the course—that having to do with the formal principles of artistic creation—but some comments are necessary with respect to the relation of formal organization to the basic problem of expression and to the various mediums of expression. Formal organization is a crucial problem for it is the means whereby medium is given articulate organization—that is to say, organization which will communicate that which the artist wishes to express. The idea alone is disembodied spirit, so to speak; medium alone, until it has been organized into a coherent pattern, is inert and inexpressive. Formal organization, therefore, is the means whereby these two factors are unified. At the same time, the particular organization of any work of art will be determined not only by the idea to be expressed but also by the medium for, as we have seen, each medium has certain possibilities and limitations for both expression and organization. It is clear, therefore, that only within certain limits can these three factors—idea, medium, and formal organization—be considered separately. Full understanding and appreciation is possible only as the very close interrelationships existing between them are comprehended.

The final phase of the course proposed here would, in a sense, constitute a recapitulation of the first two parts, but with a more pointed emphasis and a more extended treatment. It would deal more specifically with the arts as an important aspect of contemporary culture and as they enter into the life of the individual living today, and would focus on such questions as the following: What specific contributions can esthetic experience make to fuller individual and social living? What are the values of active participation in the arts? What relationship do the arts bear to each of the major areas of living? What are the potential values of the arts which are not being fully realized in our culture? How can we work toward a fuller realization of these values? It may be seen that this final phase of the course would, in a sense, be a period of evaluation in which the student would be able to bring together the understandings which he has achieved as they relate to his own life and his own culture. It may be said that the final test of the course lies in the answers which the student offers in response to these questions, for the course has achieved its purposes only if the experiences which it has provided have been significant and meaningful in his life and have given him a larger vision of the meaning and import of the arts in the life which he is living today.

Since the full values of a course such as this can be realized only as the arts are studied in direct relationship to each other, it is most necessary that the specific learning activities in the course should be planned with this in mind. Particularly to be avoided is the kind of situation in which one instructor-specialist succeeds another on the platform and each art form is dealt with in isolation from the others. There will, of course, be times when an entire class session—or perhaps several—will be devoted to one of the arts, but even in these cases there will generally be many opportunities for drawing parallels between that one art and others and for throwing it into relief against the larger background provided by the other arts. Panel discussions by the staff members are suggested as one method of maintaining a close interrelation between the various special interests represented by the staff. At other times, when a particular aspect of one of the arts can best be presented by one staff member within a given block of time, it may be well to provide some time in which the other instructors may make comments from the point of view of their particular fields. Contributions which the students make to discussions may also be counted on to help in maintaining a close relationship since the various students will generally be speaking from the point of view of the particular art forms in which they are doing laboratory work. The techniques for maintaining a desirable integration will vary considerably depending upon the particular situation—the material being discussed, the characteristics of the students, and the characteristics of the staff members. This is a problem, however, which should be constantly kept in mind, for the success with which it is handled will be a major factor in determining the success of the entire course.

The general basis for relating studio activities to the lecture-discussion sessions is provided by the basic orientation of the course to the expressive quality of the arts. For two reasons, it is difficult to make specific recommendations as to how this relationship can best be effected. In the first place, because of the differences between the arts, the exact nature of the activities in the various laboratories will differ considerably and each will have to be related in its own way to the concepts developed in the lecture-discussion sessions. In addition, because of the desirability for a high degree of individualization in the laboratory work and a maximum of student planning, specific procedures for developing relationships between laboratory and lecture-discussion activities cannot be indicated.

There are, however, two general concepts which have an important bearing on this problem. First, it is essential that the material of the lecture-discussion sections be conceived in such terms that it will have applicability to the student's laboratory activities. A discussion of mediums, for example, will have much greater meaning for the student if frequent reference is made to the problems which he is facing in his creative activities. Or a discussion of industrial design as a manifestation of our contemporary culture will be more significant if the student can see it as related to his laboratory work in designing a house, or a motorcar, or a flashlight.

In the second place, instruction in the laboratory should, wherever possible, draw upon the concepts which are developed in the lecture-discussion sessions. With reference to the basic problem of expression, as well as the problems of medium and formal principles, the possibilities for such relationships are self-evident. Examples may serve to illustrate similar possibilities in the area of cultural backgrounds of the arts. A student who is interested in house design may, through achieving a fuller understanding of the arts as reflections of the culture pattern, see the "rightness" of contemporary architecture as the solution to the problems of living which we face today. Another student interested in costume design may be inspired to make an intensive study of the dress of a particular era and to design costumes for a play set in that period. Or a group of students engaged on a project in city planning may gain new insights into their problems through an understanding of the close relationships between modern city planning and modern technology. These examples illustrate the kinds of relationships which may be developed between laboratory and lecture-discussion activities. The following chapter, limiting itself to the field of the visual arts, will discuss in greater detail the various kinds of activities appropriate to art instruction and the contributions which each can make to the total program.

Chapter X

PROBLEMS OF INSTRUCTION

TYPES OF INSTRUCTIONAL ACTIVITY IN THE ART PROGRAM

What has been said of the selection and organization of course content in the art program is equally true of the instructional activities which are pursued: that they must be judged in terms of their appropriateness to the goals toward which instruction is directed. The evaluation of any kind of activity, therefore, must be undertaken in terms of, first, what we know of the nature of human learning; second, the kind of learning which we wish to take place; and third, the fitness of the activity to the particular characteristics of the subject matter with which we are dealing.

Although in recent years its position of supremacy has been seriously questioned, the lecture method is still the one most commonly used in college instruction. This is only slightly less true in the arts than in some other areas of instruction, and there are many art courses which are taught almost entirely by the lecture method. The most serious criticism of this method of instruction is that it generally proceeds from a view of learning as absorbing rather than as building. The individual learner is regarded as a passive agent, and the information and knowledge which form the content of the lecture are *added to* that which he has previously absorbed. Psychological discoveries about the learning process have exposed the fallacy of this concept and have shown that learning is essentially a process of integration whereby the individual builds new experiences into his present understandings. Learning is growth rather than accumulation. It is the function of education not to give the student packaged ideas which he can store away side by side but rather to provide the kind of environment in which desirable growth can take place. Thus the lecture method presents a twofold difficulty: in the first place, it tends to be oriented primarily in terms of the subject matter which forms the content of the lectures rather than the students to whom the lectures are addressed; in the second place, it provides but limited opportunity for the students actively to relate the new information and ideas presented in the lectures to their present store of concepts and understandings.

It seems, therefore, that the lecture method can be used to the greatest advantage when it is related to other kinds of learning activities. There are undoubtedly some types of material which can be most effectively and efficiently presented in lecture form. And when presented by an able lecturer such material can be given a cogency which is hard to duplicate with other methods. Furthermore, lectures may be a source of stimulation which, by opening up new avenues of experience, will move the student to further activity whereby these new avenues will be more fully and meaningfully explored in terms of his own particular insights and understandings. Finally, lectures, if they are closely attuned to the learning processes of the student and to his background of experience, may be the means whereby concepts with which he has been struggling can be clarified and brought into more meaningful relationship with previous learnings.

With particular respect to instruction in the visual arts, there is a further difficulty which attends a too great use of the lecture method, arising from the fact that the art experience is essentially nonverbal. The lecture may *talk about* art in a most effective manner, but it cannot *provide* the art experience itself. Indeed, as Ducasse has indicated (see p. 170), verbalization may tend to block esthetic experience rather than facilitate it. On the other hand, a verbal approach, so long as it is clearly recognized as being purely a means toward the understanding of an entirely different kind of experience, may provide a way for leading the student from a familiar to an unfamiliar medium of expression. Furthermore, it may provide a means whereby the esthetic experience, once it has been felt, can be further clarified and understood. For example, a lecture on Surrealist painting, if it helps the student understand the essential characteristics of this kind of art and the ideas which motivate it, may, in the first place, give him a broader perspective from which to approach it, and may also give him a better understanding of his own reactions to it. Without denying the values of the lecture method, then, it is necessary that we recognize its limitations and understand that its usefulness is, to a large extent, contingent upon its relation to other types of activity which, on the one hand, provide students with the esthetic experience itself and, on the other hand, provide opportunity for the integration of new experiences into meaningful relationships.

The activity which is most commonly used to supplement lectures is the discussion method. With respect to this type of activity in art instruction, Longman has written as follows:

By means of the Socratic method the student can best learn self-confidence in judgment and acquire an intimate understanding of the material and an appropriate active vocabulary to express his experience with the fine arts. Without this, the instructor cannot be certain whether the student comprehends what is being taught. A successful general education course is not an old-fashioned Cook's tour. The student should not be compelled to swallow more than he can digest.[1]

The emphasis here seems to be on the value of the discussion as a check for the instructor on the student's comprehension of the material which has been presented. While this is no doubt of great significance to the instructor who wishes to relate his

[1] In Earl J. McGrath and others, *Toward General Education* (New York: The Macmillan Company, 1948), p. 197.

lecture material to the capacities and understandings of his students, it seems even more important to recognize that discussion can be a means whereby the student clarifies his own understandings and relates new concepts to his present and past experiences. In fact, rather than following the lecture and being subsidiary to it, discussion may provide the basis for subsequent lectures. Let us imagine, for example, that a class has engaged in a discussion of the modern artist and his relation to society. The insights into the problem which the students exhibit in their discussion, the limitations in their understanding which are revealed, and the general pattern of their thinking—that is, the kind of questions they raise and the answers they supply—will provide the instructor with valuable clues as to the nature of the material he should present in a lecture and the way in which he should present it. Subsequent discussions may then provide the students further opportunity to relate the material of the lecture to their own understandings.

With respect to instruction in the visual arts, discussion activities are subject to the same limitations as the lecture method in that they constitute a verbal approach to a nonverbal kind of experience. A verbal approach is, of course, indispensable to a complete learning situation; but while verbal facility and "an appropriate active vocabulary" may enable the student to talk about his esthetic experience, they provide no assurance of an essentially esthetic response to the arts. Care must be taken that discussion periods are not experiences in sheer verbalization which move away from, rather than toward, a deeper comprehension of the unique contributions of the arts to living.

Because experience in the visual arts is itself nonverbal, it is activities which are essentially nonverbal in nature which are most crucial to successful instruction. Such activities may be directed primarily toward the development of esthetic perception and appreciation or may be concerned primarily with actual creative expression. These two types of experience form the core and substance of all instruction in the arts and activities of a verbal nature can never be more than a means whereby the values of these nonverbal kinds of experience can be more fully explored and realized. In fostering understanding and appreciation of the visual arts and in stimulating creative activity there can be no substitute for a rich and varied visual environment. The sources of visual stimulation may include not only objects of art but any aspect of our visual world which may be esthetically rewarding. A particular type of visual experience which may be of considerable value is the demonstration of the various art processes. Such demonstrations may, on the one hand, give students insights into the creative process as, for example, watching a motion picture of Matisse painting a picture; on the other hand, the purpose of the demonstration may be primarily to orient the students in a studio class to various materials and processes with which they will be working.

Because of the particular importance of visual experience in art instruction, subsequent sections of this chapter will deal specifically with the resources for visual material both in the classroom and in the community. With respect to studio experiences as well, specific attention will be given later to some of the particular problems which it raises.

In concluding this discussion it is necessary to call attention to one further point which was alluded to in Chapter IX. This has to do with the importance of maintaining a close relationship between the various kinds of activity which are pursued in a single course. This generally presents little difficulty with respect to lectures and discussions for, in the first place, they are both verbal activities and, furthermore, discussions are generally directed toward a clarification of concepts which have been presented in the lecture. In all too many cases, however, there is no such tie between lecture-discussion sessions and studio activities and any relationships which may exist are purely fortuitous.

There are several reasons for this. In the first place, the essential difference between verbalization and studio participation makes the relationship a more difficult one to maintain. In the second place, while the lecture and discussion periods are group activities in which everyone concerned is having, at least overtly, the same kind of experience, the studio work is apt to be of a much more individualized nature with a greater variety of interests and activities. Certain administrative arrangements also tend to make the problem more difficult. There are many cases in which the course is so administered that the students taking the lecture-discussion part of the course may or may not, at their own discretion, enroll for studio work and thus any extended reference to the experience in the studio, since it can have meaning only for those who are engaged in studio activities, must be avoided. The only satisfactory solution to this problem would seem to be a separate section of the course for those not wishing to engage in studio activities. It frequently happens, furthermore, that lecture-discussion sections and studio sections are taught by separate instructors, and, through lack of adequate planning, there is a failure to relate the experiences of the two sections. It is highly desirable that all the activities of such a course be under the guidance of the same instructor, but in cases where this is not possible a relationship should be maintained through complete and careful planning. Activities which are segmented and unrelated can make no more than a partial contribution to the growth and understanding of the student. Only as all his experiences are consciously related can the maximum rewards of each individual experience be realized.

USE OF VISUAL MATERIALS

In art instruction perhaps more than any other area, the use of visual materials is important, for here the visual experience forms the center and focus of learning. Yet all too often many of the possibilities for visual stimulation are overlooked or neglected. In the first place, the instructor whose special interest is the visual arts and who has had long years of experience with them may fail to realize that the students with whom he deals do not have the same degree of visual awareness and acuteness as he possesses and are not as receptive to the visual aspects of their environment. Because of this he may frequently assume that a single example is sufficient to illustrate a point which he wishes to make whereas actually it will have much less significance and meaning for the student than it has for him because the experiences to which they are able to relate it are much more limited. In other cases the instructor may assume that the mere mention of some common aspect of the environment will be sufficient with no visual demonstration at all, whereas actually such a verbal reference may not evoke in the minds of the students the same image which the instructor has in his mind.

The material which the instructor uses, therefore, need not be limited to objects of art. The publication, *Art Forms in Nature*[2] and the more recent portfolio of the Museum of Modern Art on textures and patterns[3] give numerous examples of the visual pleasures which are a part of our everyday environment. Even such common things as feathers, shells, pieces of driftwood, beautifully shaped and colored stones, leaves, and seed pods, may introduce the students to new kinds of visual experience. Objects such as these form an invaluable source of materials for the instructor who must first of all teach his students to see the world with a fresh vision.

As for visual materials relating more specifically to the arts, there are many valuable sources at the disposal of the instructor. In many cases, reproductions, generally in the form of slides and photographs, constitute the entire range of visual material which is used. While these are unquestionably of great value, it is necessary to point out that they are frequently no more than a poor substitute for direct experience with actual objects of art. In this connection, Grimes has commented as follows:

If . . . the development of creative imagination is the important objective in teaching the appreciation of art, reproductions can be counted on to contribute little. Such materials are not of sufficient experimental value to furnish the major substance of visual materials in any study in which art appreciation is an objective. From their present dominant position in education they must be relegated to a supplementary one if teaching is actually to affect the choices and reactions people make in daily living.[4]

As possible local sources of actual art objects, Grimes lists the following: the layout of the local community, its public buildings and its homes; sculpture to be found in public build-

[2] Karl Blossfeldt, *Art Forms in Nature* (New York: E. Weyhe, 1929, 1932), 240 pl.
[3] Elodie Courter Osborn, *Texture and Pattern* (New York: Museum of Modern Art, 1949), 2 pp. + 40 pl.
[4] James Grimes, "Problems of Materials in Art Instruction," *Educational Research Bulletin*, XXIII (January, 1944), 21.

ings, churches, and cemeteries; paintings in public buildings and from the collections of private owners, clubs, and organizations; crafts made by people in the community; and the work of talented students. To this list may be added the work of local artists; the often very fine exhibits of student work which are circulated by college art departments and art schools; in larger colleges and universities, the contents of their museums and galleries; the traveling exhibits which are being circulated to an increasing extent by galleries and museums throughout the country; and the many private and public museums in the larger urban centers.

The above listing deals primarily with sources of examples in the fine arts of architecture, sculpture, and painting. If we move beyond the limits of the fine arts, the sources are even more numerous and readily at hand. The most common objects of everyday use—clothes, teacups, cigarette lighters, chairs, and lampshades—may profitably be used to illustrate the esthetic aspects of the everyday environment. Such objects as furniture, textiles, pottery, jewelry, and glassware may often be borrowed from local merchants or manufacturers, or field trips may be arranged to visit their places of business. In the fields of commercial and industrial art, there is a great wealth of illustrative material available. The advertisements in newspapers and magazines, posters and billboards, the typographic design and layout of all manner of publications, and the myriad products of industry are all at the hands of the instructor and provide an almost unlimited source of visual material.

In many areas of the arts the contacts which the average student has in his day-to-day living are predominantly with the forms of the past and so he has been powerfully conditioned to think of the arts in terms of such forms. This fact increases the need for the art program to provide as many visual experiences as possible with contemporary forms of expression. In some areas such as clothing design and certain fields of industrial design historic examples will be relatively difficult to find and instruction will have to deal almost exclusively with contemporary work. In most of the other areas, there is a wealth of materials which the instructor may draw upon for the arts of today. Most every community has in it now some examples of contemporary architecture, and magazines such as the *Architectural Forum* and *Interiors* deal almost exclusively with contemporary forms in architecture and interior design. There is a constantly growing number of slides, motion pictures, and color reproductions devoted to contemporary arts and many magazines are giving greater attention to the work of living artists. Circulating exhibitions and the work of practicing artists in the community provide sources for actual examples of the work which is being done today.

Notwithstanding their inferiority to actual objects of art, reproductions do, and probably will for some time to come, constitute the bulk of visual material used in most art courses, particularly in the area of the fine arts. With respect to most of the famous works of art, of course, instructors are faced with presenting them in reproduction or not presenting them at all, and even though they cannot be experienced in their original form it is important that students should have some contact with the best that has been produced as well as with that which is most readily available and closest to them. Furthermore, it is frequently true that such original material as is available will be quite inadequate for a complete exploration of certain areas of art. For example, in a community where most of the houses were built during the Victorian era, a study of house design which limited itself to local examples would present a most distorted and incomplete picture. Whatever may be said, therefore, about the relative inferiority of reproductions, it must be recognized that they constitute an important and essential part of the visual resources for art instruction.

While slides are perhaps the best kind of reproduction to use with classes of any size, there are other types which may be used to great advantage. The very fine color reproductions which are available today are of such a quality as to provide an experience which, if not identical, is at least similar to the experience of the original. The reproductions in art magazines and in publications such as *Life, Vogue,* and *Fortune* can provide an extensive source of material. In addition to still photographs, the motion picture is assuming increasing importance as an aid to instruction in the arts. Available productions deal with the works of particular artists as well as with demonstrations of processes and mediums in the arts. The possibilities which such films present for art instruction are manifold and have only begun to be realized.

Special mention should be made of photography as an art medium. Both the still photograph and the motion picture have been recognized as methods of reproduction for presenting material dealing with other art forms, but as art mediums in their own right they have received scant attention. In still photography, the works of such men as Steichen, Strand, and Weston are penetrating statements conceived in esthetic terms. The motion picture has received greatest attention as a form of dramatic art, but the visual possibilities of the medium, even when it carries a dramatic emphasis, are considerable. Furthermore, there is a growing number of films being produced which treat the motion picture primarily as a medium of visual expression. The abstract films of such men as Moholy-Nagy, Fischinger, and MacLaren are examples of the purely visual treatment of the medium. Other works, such as those of Maya Deren, though not abstract, have an impact which is primarily visual rather than dramatic. Because our concepts of the possibilities of the motion picture have been so dominated by the Hollywood product, with its emphasis on the dramatic element, we have scarcely realized that it is a medium with enormous possibilities for purely visual expression. In this capacity it deserves a great deal more attention than it has so far received.

THE NATURE OF STUDIO ACTIVITIES

Work in the studio can provide the student with some of his deepest and most meaningful experiences with the arts. It is therefore of especial importance that attention be given to the values which studio activities are set up to achieve and to the procedures by which these values can be most fully realized. Their most important purpose is to provide opportunity for meaningful creative activity in the visual arts, for as Edwin Ziegfeld has written, "Participation in the arts has demonstrated that it can be a potent force in helping an individual to develop self-confidence through clarifying his own feelings and beliefs, but most important, through offering individuals opportunity for some creative development. . . ." [5] In addition, there are two other purposes which studio activity may help to achieve: first, it may contribute to the student's developing awareness of the rewards of esthetic experience and a consequent reevaluation of his patterns of living in this light; and it may increase his capacity for esthetic response and evaluation through a greater familiarity with the problems of artistic creation. These purposes provide a background against which to discuss the nature of the activities pursued in the studio.

In the first place, primary emphasis should be placed on the experience which the student undergoes rather than on the product which is the result of his activities. In this connection, Ziegfeld has written that "In order to satisfy [the] need for creative activity the product need not be of professional quality; in fact, the product is of less importance than what happens to the person while it is being made." [6] While it is true that for the student the product will generally be of great importance, as far as the instructor is concerned this interest in the product should be viewed as another manifestation of the experience which the student is undergoing. The development of skill as an end in itself may have an important place in some courses for professional artists, but it is quite inappropriate to the laboratory activities of the general student. Here skill is always subservient and instrumental to his desire for expression.

It may be worth while here to recall the earlier discussion of the relation of self-expression to the creative act (pp. 90–91). It was pointed out that the individual expresses himself through expressing his unique view of the world. He does not, as Buermeyer says, "luxuriate in his own feelings"; he is oriented toward the world in which he lives and as this world passes through the channel of his feelings it emerges in a form which is expressive of him as an individual. An overemphasis on self-

[5] Edwin Ziegfeld, "The College Art Program in General Education," *Journal of General Education*, II (April, 1948), 243–44.
[6] *Ibid.*, p. 244.

expression, therefore, may be dangerous in that it will encourage a self-conscious introspection—a greater concern with the individual's own self than with the world as perceived by that self.

Lest the foregoing statements be taken to mean that the student is always bursting with ideas for creative expression, it must be quickly added that this is certainly not the case. In all too many instances, the powerful pressures of a conservative and traditional environment—and with respect to the arts, often a second- or third-rate environment—have resulted in hackneyed and stereotyped forms of expression. It is one of the most difficult tasks that the instructor faces to help the student break through his inhibitions, to move away from his stereotyped concepts toward a view of the world which is his own—which is genuinely original and creative. The techniques used by various instructors to encourage freedom and originality of expression will vary considerably, but there are several general principles which are applicable to at least the great majority of cases.

The first point to be emphasized is the importance of respecting and fostering the integrity of the student's response and expression. Although his vision and his purposes may, according to the instructor's lights, be limited or even in error, they represent his best efforts and, more important, they are the only basis on which he has to build. The help and criticism which are offered by the instructor must be framed in terms of the purposes which the student is trying to achieve to help him arrive at a more adequate expression of the thing he wants to say the way he wants to say it. While his present purposes may be extremely limited, they must provide the basis for further growth; he has to move from where he is at the present moment, not from where the instructor is. The instructor must steer an uneasy course between destroying the student's self-confidence and encouraging a smug satisfaction with his present accomplishments.

A second point has to do with the importance of a stimulating environment. New experiences beget the desire for more new experiences. If the studio itself provides stimulation—in the activities which are being carried on, in the ideas which are presented, in the visual experiences provided—by that much the motivation of the students will be increased. With respect to the visual environment in the studio, it should be mentioned that it is hardly enough merely to change the bulletin board every day or to put up a new exhibit once a week. Students whose vision has been dulled through years of disuse need help in seeing. Unless their attention is directed specifically to new objects in the room, to exhibits, and to bulletin board displays, and unless they are helped to see them and to evaluate them, the potential value of such materials will not be realized.

Another important source of stimulation is provided by the art materials in the studio. Small children are naturally curious about materials and eager to experiment with them and manipulate them. Frequently, by the time we have reached adulthood, or even late adolescence, we have lost much of our curiosity—and our courage—and our tendency to take things for granted robs us of many experiences of discovery and exploration. By reawakening an interest in materials and a desire to experiment with them, to manipulate them, to see what they can do and what they can't do, the instructor can encourage creative discoveries in artistic expression. The studio, therefore, should be equipped with as great a range as possible of art materials, and students should be encouraged to experiment with them, to find what their qualities are—their possibilities and their limitations for creative expression.

At the same time, granted the importance of a wide variety of materials, there is probably no single material or medium which must of necessity be experienced by all the students. There is often the tendency to feel that studio courses of this kind have failed unless they have given each student experience in clay, in oil paint, in water color, in woodworking, and so on. The position taken here is that the specific materials with which the student works are of much less importance than the kind of experience he has with them. One individual may derive the greatest satisfaction from working with clay but may feel hampered and ill-at-ease with a water-color brush, while another may feel most at home with water color but be quite incapable of satisfactory achievement in a three-dimensional medium.

Against the values of variety of experience must be measured the values of depth of experience.

A final point to be emphasized with respect to studio work is the importance of helping the student to use his own creative activities in extending and refining his capacities for esthetic response and appreciation. An experience with color may or may not help the student to have a finer appreciation of the paintings of Matisse; whether or not this is the case will depend largely upon whether the instructor helps him to see the relationship between his own experiences and the color statements in Matisse's paintings. Likewise, a student who is interested in house design may, by studying the solutions which modern architects have devised for contemporary living, not only be stimulated in his own work but also gain a greater appreciation and understanding of contemporary domestic architecture. Only as due attention is given to both the doing and the undergoing aspects of esthetic experience can the full benefits of studio experiences be realized.

RELATING INSTRUCTION TO STUDENT NEEDS AND INTERESTS

The importance of this concept has already been pointed out with reference to the selection and organization of course content. It is of equal importance with respect to the activities which are pursued in the specific classroom situation. In this connection, Alberty has written as follows:

What we know about the nature of the individual and learning suggests that optimal learning takes place when the individual acts with reference to his interests, his recognized needs, and his own pattern of values. This is not to say that the school accepts his goals as satisfactory and valid. It must help him to evaluate his behavior, to create new interests, to sense neglected aspects of growth as well as to reconstruct his patterns of goals.[7]

Although it is essential to give due regard to the latter part of Alberty's statement, the importance of the student's purposes

[7] Harold Alberty, *Reorganizing the High School Curriculum* (New York: The Macmillan Company, 1948), pp. 47–48.

and interests may be seen as central to the learning process. While one of the college's first obligations is to lead toward the improving of student goals, it has an equal obligation to recognize and respect the student's present goals and interests, for only as it does this can it insure effective learning and the development of worthy purposes.

As a specific example, a study of the graphic arts as a means of communication may begin with the hieroglyphic drawings of the Egyptians, proceed from there to the story-telling functions of Medieval art, and so on to the political satire of Daumier's lithographs. An approach more closely attuned to the student's present purposes and interests might begin with a consideration of the comic strip as a medium of communication and proceed from this familiar beginning to a study of forms more remote from his immediate experience. Likewise, a study of community architecture may begin with the Roman Forum or the Doge's Palace in Venice; on the other hand, it may begin with a visit to the city hall in one's own community. Such an approach enables the student to evaluate new experiences in terms of what he already knows and feels and to build with greater confidence on his present knowledge and experience.

This would seem to be the most effective way of moving the student along to a continually higher level of taste and appreciation, for his growth will be more definitely assured if his new experiences originate from familiar territory. For example, if a student has thought of the art of painting only in terms of its representational or story-telling function, merely to tell him that this is a relatively unimportant consideration in modern painting may antagonize him, confuse him, or destroy his confidence in his own judgment. If, on the other hand, he can be shown why story-telling has, at certain periods in history and for certain groups, been an important function of painting and what conditions in our contemporary culture have operated to make it less important, there is a greater possibility that he will be able to reframe his original concepts of painting in terms of a larger background. He may also be shown that even those artists who have given great attention to representation or the telling of a story have been even more concerned with other problems of a purely artistic nature and that modern painters, concerned with the same problems, are merely solving them in a contemporary idiom.

It is also true, of course, that the sudden, and perhaps shocking, impact of a completely new experience may frequently jar the student out of a complacent acceptance of his present values and attitudes. But even here the new experience must in some way be related to what he already knows and feels even if the relationship is purely one of contrast. It is one of the skills of teaching to know what kinds of experiences will most effectively reach a student or a group. It seems certain that only as new experiences can be related to past and present ones will learning take place.

PROVISION FOR STUDENT PARTICIPATION IN PLANNING ACTIVITIES

Students should not only be able to see the relevance of learning activities to their own interests and goals; they should also have an active part in planning the activities in which they participate. Krug has enumerated six questions which must be answered in connection with any and all curriculum planning:

Why?   This question may be ignored only at one's peril.

What?   This brings up the question of content of instruction.

When?   This involves time scheduling, preparation of a calendar, or agenda. When you start a unit of work, you and your group need to anticipate the "when" question to some extent or you simply won't come out.

Who?   Even if all the students read the same twenty pages for tomorrow's lesson, that's one kind of answer to this. But if we don't always have all the students doing the same thing, somebody has to decide who is going to do what—and when.

How?   This brings up the whole question of choice of activities.

Where?   Often this question is answered by saying, "In the classroom." But this isn't always the answer. There are the school library, the community . . . etc.[8]

[8] Edward A. Krug, *Curriculum Planning* (New York: Harper and Brothers, 1950), pp. 200–01.

The extent to which students will be able to work effectively in answering these questions will depend largely upon whether or not the entire course has been structured in relation to their interests and understandings. In the first place, their desire to participate in the planning of activities will correspond closely with the interest which they feel and exhibit. In the second place, their ability to plan effectively will depend upon the extent to which the goals being pursued are goals which they can understand and to which they can intelligently relate their plans.

It is in individual studio work that such planning can be most easily carried on. But this is not the only kind of activity which can be planned by the students. To begin with, group projects in studio work offer rich possibilities for student initiative and planning. Examples of such projects in which the students can be given the major responsibility for planning and execution are: the arrangement and decoration of classrooms, the design and execution of murals, the production of exhibits, and the production and illustration of class publications. The kinds of collaborative projects, suggested in Chapter IX (p. 164), which involve students from several areas of the arts offer rich possibilities for student planning.

Within the framework of the course organization which was suggested in Chapter IX, many opportunities could be developed for student planning in connection with the lecture-discussion sessions. Each of the areas of emphasis suggested has sufficient breadth and flexibility so that the problems involved could be studied in a great variety of ways and the students could take an active part in planning the specific activities to be carried out. It is true that an integrated course of the kind suggested generally involves a large number of students, a fact which increases the difficulties of student planning. One possible way of meeting this problem would be for planning activities to be initiated in the small laboratory groups. The lecture-discussion session would then provide an opportunity for pooling the ideas of the various groups, and out of this the final plans would be developed. The small groups might also plan presentations to be made to the total class. A specific example of this kind of activity may be given. An integrated course in the arts was divided into small discussion groups each of which was given the responsibility for making a final presentation to the entire class. The group interested in the dance decided to organize an exhibit, the idea of which was to illustrate the basic similarities and differences between modern dance and the other major art forms. The entire project was planned and executed by the students themselves. In carrying it out, they not only increased their understanding of the modern dance but also gained greater familiarity with the other mediums of artistic expression. By utilizing student interest and initiative in this way the activities of both the classroom and the studio can be given added meaning and will result in richer and deeper learning experiences.

UTILIZING RESOURCES OUTSIDE THE CLASSROOM

The foregoing discussion has already suggested the importance of utilizing the college and the community as sources of visual materials. There are, in addition, a number of other ways in which both the college and the outside community may be used to enrich the art program. Because each situation will vary in the resources which are available, it is possible here only to suggest some of the more common possibilities. Generally, in other departments of the college or in the community there are individuals who, because of their special interests and experiences, may be able to contribute to the art program. In addition to instructors in other areas of the arts, there are anthropologists, sociologists, psychologists, and estheticians, among the staff members who may be called upon to talk with the students from their particular points of view. While it is true that there are frequently many difficulties standing in the way of this kind of interchange between departments of the college, the possibilities which such activities offer deserve to be explored more than they have been in the past. Not only can the art department profit from such contributions by staff members from outside; it can also, in many cases, give a like service to other departments.

Another valuable kind of experience may be gained by taking the students out into the community. Mention has already been made of the resources which every community offers for the study of city planning, architecture, and to a lesser degree, painting and sculpture. But this by no means exhausts the possibilities. A visit to a textile plant, for example, might be arranged for a group of students who are interested in weaving or textile design. In connection with activities in graphic processes or book design, students could broaden their understanding by taking a trip through a printing establishment. Or a local pottery might be a valuable source of learning for students interested in ceramics.

Both the college and the community may provide opportunities for many worth-while student projects. On the campus, the list of such possibilities would include the development of visual aids for other departments, working with students in other departments on the design and production of exhibits, design and execution of posters for campus activities, and working with student organizations on various art problems which they may encounter. In most cases, it is true, the college art department does not need to look far for such opportunities and the requests for services are apt to be numerous. Sometimes the work to be done is of negligible educational value or the request is made on such short notice that it is impossible to utilize it as a learning activity for the students. While services of this kind may be most valuable from a public relations standpoint and may be undertaken for this reason, they can become a burden of some proportions. At other times, the kind of work to be done is beyond the capabilities of the students in this kind of course, and, if it is attempted, results only in dissatisfaction for all the parties concerned. It is essential, therefore, that the various opportunities which present themselves should be carefully evaluated in terms of the contributions they will make to the growth of the students and should be pursued as studio projects only if they give promise of substantial rewards in terms of student learning.

Projects similar to those just described may also be developed in the community. For example, local merchants may be persuaded to allow students to take the responsibility for decorating their show windows. City beautification projects offer another possibility for student participation. In one town, the officials of the municipal heating plant called upon members of the art staff in the local school system to help plan colors for the interior of the plant and this provided an interesting problem for students in the art classes. Festivals and carnivals sponsored by business and civic groups may offer many challenges to the students in the planning of decorations, the design of floats and costumes, and the design of carnival booths.

Finally, it is often possible to secure excellent materials for laboratory use from local manufacturers and merchants. Scraps of linoleum and lumber, waste materials from paper plants or from factories which fabricate metals, discarded textile samples, scraps of leather and of felt are examples of the kinds of materials which may often be secured free or at a nominal cost. With respect to materials as well as all the other resources mentioned above, each community will have different possibilities. It is the job of the resourceful instructor to discover what his particular community will yield.

Chapter XI

PROBLEMS OF ADMINISTRATION

ADMINISTERING THE ART COURSE

SHALL WORK IN THE ARTS BE REQUIRED?

The problem of elective courses versus required courses is a difficult one and there are strong arguments in favor of both positions. It has been stated earlier that every individual has the capacity and the need for esthetic experience and expression and that failure to meet this need results in an incomplete and distorted development. It might seem, therefore, that, particularly in a society such as ours where the validity of esthetic experience is so little realized, we should require without exception that every student in our colleges have a minimum of course work in the arts.

On the other hand, the very strong resistance which is felt by many students to the entire field of the arts may often operate largely to vitiate any possible advantages which they might otherwise gain from taking work in the arts. For both students and staff members there is often a stigma attached to required courses. Students, even though they may not be antagonistic to a particular field of study, are moved to resistance as soon as they are told that they must take a course. Staff members, because they must deal with students who are in the course under pressure and who openly show their antagonism and lack of interest, approach their work with something less than enthusiasm.

In the arts particularly this is a crucial point because of the very nature of the art experience. While it is true that any kind of learning is influenced deeply by the attitude and the emotional tone of the student, this factor is of particular importance in the arts because, in the first place, the art experience itself is largely a matter of the emotions. Furthermore, the essentially creative nature of participative activity in the arts demands a kind of free and spontaneous behavior which grows out of the student's own interest and enthusiasm.

However, in addition to the argument stated above, there are other important points in favor of requiring work in the arts. First, there are many students who, out of indifference rather than dislike, will not elect courses in art. This may be the result of several factors: it may be based on their unfamiliarity with the arts and a consequent lack of understanding of the rewards of art experience; it may be in response to the natural impulse to avoid the unfamiliar in favor of better-known subjects where there is more security and a greater certainty of success; or there may be pressures from many sources in the college or in the students' personal life which lead them to omit the arts from their programs. There is another group of students who feel a real interest in the arts and a desire for art experience but whose timidity and lack of confidence will discourage them from electing art courses. They share the wide-held misconception that ability in the arts is limited to a select few and are fearful of attempting work in an area for which they do not have "special talent."

Finally, it must be recognized that in the great majority of colleges today there are course requirements in almost all the other subject-matter fields. Within such a situation, an art program which is set up on a completely elective basis is working against insuperable odds. There is little hope that it can hold its own in competition with required courses or that it can adequately serve the needs of the college.

Clearly, to require work in the arts greatly increases the necessity for devising courses which are closely geared to the felt needs and interests of the students. This implies not only a change in focus for many courses but also a much more flexible kind of organization which will be adaptable to a great diversity of interests and capacities. Requiring work in the arts demands more rather than less effort to help the students understand the relevance of such experience to their own living. This can be achieved not only in the classroom but through various activities in the campus community. The informal contacts in a campus community which is rich in opportunities for art experience will result inevitably in a more widespread interest on the part of the students. A subsequent section of this chapter will deal with the kinds of campus activities which should be included in the arts program.

The final aspect of this problem to be mentioned is the need for an adequate system of individual counseling in the college program. The inexperienced student coming to college is frequently confused as to his own purposes and interests and has little if any knowledge about the varied offerings of the college program. It can hardly be expected, therefore, that without help he will be able to see the relevance of these offerings to his own goals. With particular respect to the arts, the adviser can help the student toward a clearer assessment of his own interests and capabilities, can perhaps help him to see the values of art experience in terms of this assessment, and then can help him to determine what kind of art experiences will be best adapted to his particular interests and capabilities. To be sure, this is an ideal which we are far from realizing in most colleges. It involves, in the first place, a much more extensive counseling program than many colleges offer at the present time. Equally important, it necessitates greater understanding than many counselors possess with respect to the significance of the arts in general education. This, however, serves only to emphasize the essential interrelatedness of all the aspects of a sound general education and the great need for staff members who have breadth of vision and understanding.

SCHEDULING THE COURSE

There are two questions which must be answered with respect to this problem. The first has to do with the amount of time to be devoted to the course; the second, with the distribution of the time. The decision as to the amount of time to be given to the arts course must be made in terms of the time necessary to achieve the desired goals as well as the proportion of the student's program which can reasonably be devoted to this aspect of his education. It is felt that the minimum time allotment for a course such as the one outlined in Chapter IX would be six hours a week for one academic year. Assuming that the student, during a two-year period devoted to general education, would complete a total of sixty semester points of work, this course, carrying four points each semester, would represent about thirteen percent of his total program during this two-year period. This does not seem an unreasonable amount of time to be devoted to his esthetic education.

In most cases it would probably be more feasible, from the administrative standpoint, to extend the course over a full year than to telescope it into a single semester by doubling the number of hours per week. There is another important reason for the superiority of this time distribution. Because experience in the arts is so largely a matter of feeling and attitude, the kind of change in behavior which is the goal of art instruction often cannot be effected in a short time. A longer time span therefore seems preferable to a very concentrated course.

The most desirable time distribution within the student's weekly program would consist of two three-hour periods. Normally, one hour of each period would be devoted to lecture and discussion activities and the other two hours would be spent in the laboratory. This would mean that in an integrated course including several of the arts, all of the laboratory sections would be meeting at the same time. There are several notable advantages to such an arrangement. To begin with, the proximity in time between the lecture-discussion period and the laboratory period tends to encourage a closer relationship between them. Such an arrangement also provides a maximum of flexibility. At some times lectures may be followed immediately by extended discussion. At other times the lecture-discussion period may be dispensed with and the entire three-hour period will be spent in the laboratory. In an integrated course, collaborative projects involving students in several areas can be more easily carried out if all the laboratory sections are meeting at the same time. Finally, the three-hour block of time greatly facilitates the planning of field trips.

One final point with respect to scheduling remains to be mentioned. It frequently occurs that in courses covering two semesters students are allowed to enroll at the beginning of either semester. This, it is felt, can be done only at great cost in terms of the values which the student may realize from the course. So far as individual studio work is concerned it does not present a major problem, but with respect to activities involving the entire group it imposes a heavy penalty on the student. He is thrust into the middle of an episode the beginning of which he does not know, the direction of which he can only guess, and the end of which he can only partially understand. It is highly desirable, therefore, that all students should experience the course in the intended sequence.

GENERAL CAMPUS ACTIVITIES

In addition to formal instruction, a complete college program in the arts should include activities which are available to the entire student body as a part of their out-of-class life, as well as to other members of the college community. Some of these activities will fall under the direct control and jurisdiction of the art department. Often, however, they will be administered by another department of the college or by a student activities office, in which case it is important that some provision be made so that the art department will have a part in planning the activities.

Foremost among such activities is an art workshop which is open to all interested students whether or not they are enrolled in art courses. In fact, the primary purpose of such a workshop is to meet the needs of students who are not taking course work in the arts. Under the supervision of an instructor, the art studio is open at specified times during the week for these students to pursue their interests in art. The range of activities to be included in such a program may be extremely varied and should be limited only by the facilities which are available. In addition to the immediate rewards which students may realize from such a workshop, one of its chief values lies in the fact that it may often attract students with only a perfunctory interest in the arts who come to the workshop because they have a specific problem to solve. In the course of working on this problem, the varied activities to which they are exposed may serve to broaden and deepen their interest and lead to a reevaluation of the arts in relation to their own patterns of values.

Another important contribution which the art workshop can make is in providing stimulating activities for staff members in other subject-matter areas and thereby increasing their awareness of the importance of esthetic experience in living. Reference has already been made to the fact that a completely adequate program of instruction in the arts and an enrollment commensurate with the importance of the arts necessitates an understanding and appreciation on the part of the entire staff of the contributions which art can make to the lives of students (p. 210). Such understanding may be greatly enhanced by engaging the interest of staff members through creative activities in an informal workshop such as the one suggested here.

Another important activity which will generally reach a wider group than a workshop is an exhibit program. Many of the sources for art exhibits have already been suggested (p. 195). It should be mentioned here that a program of exhibits designed for the entire student body must cover a wide range in order to tap as great a variety of interests as possible. Exhibits of useful objects of distinguished design can generally be counted upon to attract widespread interest; collections of photographs, an occasional hobby show, exhibits dealing with interior design and costume design are other possibilities. In one case an interesting exhibit was organized from household furnishings and art objects which had been collected by the founders of the university. Another exhibit at the same university dealt with the building program which was just then getting under way.

An important aspect of any exhibit program in a college, of course, should be the work done by students enrolled in art courses. One especially effective device is the "retrospective" exhibit of work done by students while they have been enrolled, with emphasis on the growth and development which they have undergone. Such exhibits may be of especial value in stimulating the interest of a wide group of students who may be encouraged, through seeing them, to undertake some work in the arts.

An exhibit program embracing a variety of areas and closely attuned to the interests of the young people in the college can be counted upon to attract, and thus to serve, a much larger proportion of the student body than one which is limited just to the fine arts. Moreover, it may overcome the initial prejudice which students often feel toward art exhibits and lead to a more genuine acceptance of art in all its aspects.

Another possibility for an all-campus program in the arts is a loan collection of prints. This may be handled by the art department, by the library, or by the art gallery in those cases where the gallery has its own staff. For a small fee the student may borrow a reproduction of a painting for use in his own living quarters. As compared with exhibitions, this has the advantage that it enables the student to stay with one or two paintings for a long period of time and get to know them well.

Other features which may be included in the campus activities program include lecture series, theater and dance productions, and motion pictures. The lectures may be given by members of the staff or by visiting speakers and should, of course, cover a wide range of subjects. It is important, however, that the arts should be represented and that the art department should work with the agency responsible for the program in selecting and recruiting speakers. All of the activities which have been mentioned here should be regarded as a part of a unified program in the arts which is designed, not for a small group with a highly specialized interest in the arts, but for the cultural enrichment of the entire student body.

PROBLEMS OF STAFF

One of the most important administrative problems in any instructional department is the recruiting of staff members. The present discussion will attempt to indicate the training, the attitudes and philosophy, and the interests which are desirable in staff members whose primary concern will be with the arts in the general education program.

It is essential, first of all, that instructors in this area should see the relevance of art instruction to the total program of general education. Stated in terms of the student, this means that the instructor must have strong convictions with respect to the importance of art experience as an integral part of a full and satisfying life. In contrast to this attitude may be cited the case of the instructor who spoke of the general student as one with a "peripheral" interest in the arts. The point of view which is necessary for successful teaching in this area is that esthetic experience, whether for the bond salesman or the social worker, is integral, and not peripheral, to full growth and development of the personality.

This means that the instructor's interest in the arts must be balanced by a genuine and abiding interest in people and a desire to help them grow. There is a tendency in some institutions to select instructors in the arts primarily on the basis of their professional standing as practicing artists rather than their qualifications as teachers *per se*. While many such individuals may be excellent teachers, there is the very great danger that they will approach teaching from the standpoint of the specialist and that their primary interest will be the subject they are teaching rather than the students they are teaching. In general, therefore, it seems desirable to recruit staff members from the group who regard themselves primarily as teachers rather than professional artists, and whose backgrounds include a substantial amount of training in the field of education.

At the same time, it is of the utmost importance that instructors in this area should have had considerable experience in creative activity. The best way to understand the contributions which creative activity in the arts can make to individual growth is to have experienced it oneself. Because of the major role assigned to participative experience in the program recommended here, a first-hand knowledge of the creative process is vitally important. Moreover, a wide and varied background in the various mediums of the arts is essential. Because of the importance of broadening the art program to meet the needs of a highly diversified group of students, the instructor who has specialized intensively in one area of the arts to the exclusion of others will be seriously handicapped in dealing adequately with all the areas of the arts which should be included in this type of program. While it is rarely, if ever, possible to find individuals who have had experience with all the mediums of the arts, a relatively wide background is essential; and with it must be a widespread interest which will engender a desire to learn about new mediums as they are necessary for successful teaching in the area.

In addition to a broad experience in the visual arts, it is important that instructors in the general education area have some acquaintance with the other major fields of the arts. This assumes particular importance in an integrated course where the success of the course will depend, to a considerable extent, upon the ability of the various instructors to relate their fields. Only rarely will it be possible to find individuals who have a very extended knowledge of more than one, or possibly two, fields. But this scarcely seems necessary. A general acquaintance with the other arts and an interest in them should provide a sufficient basis on which the combined staff can build the kind of common understanding necessary for successful operation of an integrated course.

This introduces another characteristic which is of particular importance for instructors working in an integrated course. Because the success of such a course depends so much upon cooperative planning and the kind of give-and-take which is essential for the development of a common understanding and approach, it is necessary that the staff members should have the ability to work closely with other people and the flexibility necessary for cooperative endeavor. While this is an important characteristic in any teacher, it takes on added significance in a course which involves a number of instructors and which can succeed only as they are able to work together constructively.

PLANT AND FACILITIES

Because instruction in the visual arts makes special demands with respect to plant and facilities, specific attention must be given to this problem. It is true, of course, that worth-while art experiences can be provided in situations which offer but very limited facilities, but it is essential that there should be a certain minimum of physical equipment if the program is to be more than a meager skeleton. The present discussion will indicate the special equipment and materials which are necessary for a completely adequate program in the visual arts.

In any kind of art course, whether or not it involves studio activity, a necessary requirement is a large stock of visual materials. This would include slides—preferably color slides in those areas where color is an important factor—a slide projector, and a screen; a file of mounted photographs and color reproductions which may be secured from a wide variety of sources as indicated in Chapter IX; if possible, some large framed color reproductions; and as large a collection as possible of actual art objects. With respect to this last item, the objects need not—indeed, should not—be limited to examples of the fine arts; many objects of daily use can be valuable additions to the collection of visual materials and a buying trip to the ten-cent store may yield many items which are useful aids to instruction. Finally, because of the growing importance of the motion picture both as an art medium and as an aid to instruction, it is highly desirable that a motion picture projector should be included in the equipment of the art department, or that one should be available whenever necessary.

There are certain physical requirements which are essential in an art studio for successful teaching. To begin with, it must be a well-lighted room large enough to accommodate a variety of activities. The equipment in the room should include large work tables, drawing horses and easels, and there should be running water with a large sink. Other items which are desirable but not absolutely essential would include a small letter press for linoleum-block printing, a drying cabinet for work in clay, a potter's wheel, power equipment for woodworking such as a jigsaw and a wood lathe, and equipment for silk screen printing. An etching press and a lithographic press might also be included but are by no means vital to a successful program. It is essential that there should be storage space adequate to accommodate the large amount and variety of tools and materials involved in studio work. The room must also have generous bulletin board space for displaying visual aids and student work.

Tools and materials in the studio should include those which are necessary for the following kinds of work: drawing and painting in the various mediums such as chalk, charcoal, crayon, water color, oil, tempera, and casein paint; linoleum-block printing; clay modeling; casting and carving in plaster; wood sculpture and carving; work in wire sculpture and mobiles; work in papier-mâché; simple projects in metalwork; and the construction of models. Other types of activity which might be provided for but are not strictly essential to a successful program would include weaving, silk screen printing, etching, and lithography. It is impossible to make any very definite statements about which of the materials indicated are absolutely necessary for a successful program beyond the bare minimum necessary for painting, drawing, and some experiences in three-dimensional work. It would obviously be unwise to say that a program cannot be initiated unless all the materials indicated here are available, for if instructor and students together use their ingenuity very rich experiences can often develop out of situations which offer the most meager facilities. However, it seems certain that as the possibilities of work in different mediums are increased the values of the course will be increased correspondingly, for it will be possible to tap a much wider variety of interests and provide the opportunity for the development of special aptitudes and abilities.

Finally, it is essential that the art department have adequate space for exhibits and the equipment necessary for the attractive mounting of them. The space should have a good deal of flexibility so that it may accommodate the showing of many different kinds of material. Because the lighting of exhibitions is of major importance, there should be good general lighting and also a number of movable lights—spotlights and floodlights—which can be adjusted to meet changing requirements. Other pieces of equipment should include screens, pedestals and platforms for exhibiting three-dimensional objects, and textiles for backgrounds.

For two reasons, it is desirable that the space should be within the art department proper. In the first place, it greatly facilitates the use of the exhibitions in teaching activities. Moreover, it simplifies the problems connected with the administration of the exhibits when this is the responsibility of the art department. At the same time, the space should be situated so that it will be easily accessible to the entire student body, for an exhibition program should serve not only the art department but the staff and students of the entire college.

CONCLUSION

Current developments in our world today make it abundantly clear that the struggle for human freedom has not yet been won. The free and democratic way of life to which we in America aspire is being threatened from within and without by ideologies which would enslave the human personality and reduce the individual to subservience and anonymity. The struggle to preserve and extend our rights as free men cannot be won alone in the council chamber and on the battlefield however important our victories there may be in shaping our destiny. In order to maintain our rights to freedom we must have a spirit of freedom—a deep and abiding faith in the integrity of the individual and in his ability to build a worthy life with his fellow men. And we must have a knowledge of freedom—a true comprehension of the spontaneous and creative way of life which is the mark of the free man. Even without the threat of competing ideologies, we cannot hope to maintain a democratic way of life unless our people have faith in it and are able to live it. Against such threats, this faith and understanding are our only sure defense. To kindle such a spirit of freedom and to build the understanding out of which it develops is the foremost task of education today.

The present study has attempted to show the importance of the arts in developing a full understanding and appreciation of esthetic experience as an integral part of that free and spontaneous living which is the ideal of the democratic faith. Without the esthetic factor of experience, the individual can neither live a full life nor can he see his own life in its full relationships to the world in which he lives. Experience in the arts can give him the insights and understandings which will enable him to see himself and the world in their wholeness and fullness, and it provides him the means whereby he can relate himself freely and spontaneously—that is to say, creatively—to the world as it is given to him through his esthetic vision.

One might define democratic living by saying that it is creative living. At the same time, esthetic experience is essentially creative, for, as we have seen, it is a process by which the individual reintegrates his own experiences into new and emotionally significant patterns. A conclusion that democratic living and esthetic living are therefore synonymous would certainly be unfounded. However, it may be concluded that esthetic experience is an essential and integral element in the kind of life which democracy aspires to, that it is one of the most significant aims of democracy and an indispensable means for achieving a democratic way of life. This view is corroborated by MacMurray in the following statement:

The supreme condemnation of a civilization is that it is inartistic, that is to say, impersonal, inhuman, unreal. The absence of art is the absence of spontaneity, of proper humanity; the penalty for it is an inner stultification, a loss of spiritual integrity, a slowing down of the pulses of the inner life. We become ghosts to ourselves and to others. A civilization that has lost the capacity of the artist is a prey to spiritual paralysis, to an inner rotting of its human powers.[1]

If the purpose of general education is to foster rich and satisfying living, to give the individual a whole view of himself and of his world, and to foster a creative and spontaneous approach to the business of living—in short, to make of him a free man— then the arts must be given a more prominent and secure place in

[1] John MacMurray, *Reason and Emotion*, pp. 167–68. Copyright, 1938, D. Appleton-Century Company, Inc.

the educational program. We can no longer afford to regard them as of little consequence; the tragic results of such indifference make themselves evident in warped and distorted living which is without vision and without purpose. A full release of esthetic capacities, of free and spontaneous behavior which has the warmth of human personality and the vitality of human emotion, can open new vistas for the future of our society. Until the arts attain their full stature as an indispensable part of a full life—indeed, as a way of life—the objectives of our free society will not have been realized. As we build them into our living, we will build a strong bulwark against the enslavement of the human personality and the forces which today threaten our right to live with dignity and freedom.

Bibliography

BIBLIOGRAPHY

BIBLIOGRAPHY

ADAMS, PHILLIP R. "Fine Arts in Liberal Education." *Association of American Colleges Bulletin*, XXXIV (May, 1948), 234-41.

ADLER, MORTIMER J. "In Defense of the Philosophy of Education." *Philosophies of Education*. Forty-first Yearbook of the National Society for the Study of Education, Part I. Chicago: The Society, 1942. Pp. 197-249.

ALBERTY, HAROLD. *Reorganizing the High School Curriculum*. New York: The Macmillan Company, 1947. Pp. x + 458.

American Institute of Public Opinion. *The Gallup Political Almanac for 1948*. Princeton: The Institute, 1948.

ARRAGON, R. F. "The Arts Program at Reed College." *Association of American Colleges Bulletin*, XXVII (May, 1941), 247-51.

BAKER, GERTRUDE M. "An Enterprise in Art Appreciation with College Students." *Education*, LX (November, 1939), 162-65.

BALDINGER, WALLACE S. "The Introductory Course in Art." *College Art Journal*, II (March, 1943), 80-84.

BARR, ALFRED H. "Modern Art Makes History Too." *College Art Journal*, I (November, 1941), 3-6.

BASILIUS, H. A. "An Open Letter Addressed to the Dean of an Arts College." *Journal of Higher Education*, XVI (November, December, 1945), 424-31, 472-78.

BEESLEY, PATRICIA. *The Revival of the Humanities in American Education*. New York: Columbia University Press, 1940. Pp. xiv + 201.

BENEDICT, RUTH. *Patterns of Culture*. Boston: Houghton Mifflin Co., 1934. Pp. xiv + 291.

Bennington College. "Announcement for the Year." *Bennington College Bulletin*, XIX (July, 1950), 59.

BIGELOW, KARL W. "The Challenge of Art in a Time of Crisis." *Art Education in a Free Society*. 1947 Yearbook of the Eastern Arts Association. Kutztown: The Association, 1947. Pp. 33–46.

BIGELOW, KARL W. AND MACLEAN, MALCOLM S. "Dominant Trends in General Education." *General Education in the American College*. Thirty-eighth Yearbook of the National Society for the Study of Education, Part II. Bloomington: Public Schools Publishing Co., 1939. Pp. 351–380.

BLOSSFELDT, KARL. *Art Forms in Nature*. 2 vols. New York: E. Weyhe, 1929, 1932. 240 pl.

BOAS, GEORGE. "The Social Responsibility of the Artist." *College Art Journal*, VI (Summer, 1947), 270–76.

BRUBACHER, JOHN S. *Modern Philosophies of Education*. New York: McGraw-Hill Book Co., 1939. Pp. xiv + 370.

BUERMEYER, LAURENCE. *Aesthetic Experience*. Merion: The Barnes Foundation Press, 1929. Pp. 188.

BUTTS, R. FREEMAN. *The College Charts Its Course*. New York: McGraw-Hill Book Co., 1939. Pp. xvi + 464.

CARPENTER, MARJORIE K. "The Humanities Course at Stephens College." *College Art Journal*, II (November, 1942), 11–13.

Cooperative Study in General Education. *Cooperation in General Education*. Washington: American Council on Education, 1947. Pp. 240.

DEWEY, JOHN. *Art as Experience*. New York: Minton, Balch and Co., 1934. Pp. xii + 355.

———. *Democracy and Education*. New York: The Macmillan Company, 1916. Pp. xii + 434.

DIX, LESTER. "Art in Inter-Cultural Education." *Education*, LXVI (February, 1946), 343–49.

———. *A Charter for Progressive Education*. New York: Bureau of Publications, Teachers College, Columbia University, 1939. Pp. 107.

DORNER, ALEXANDER. *The Way Beyond "Art."* New York: Wittenborn, Schultz, Inc., 1947. Pp. 244.

DUCASSE, C. S. "Art Appreciation and the Curriculum." *Association of American Colleges Bulletin*, XXVII (October, 1941), 429–33.

DUNKEL, H. B. *General Education in the Humanities*. Washington: American Council on Education, 1947. Pp. 321.

EDMAN, IRWIN. "Art as Education." Paper read before the Committee on Art Education, New York City, May, 1950.

———. *Arts and the Man*. New York: W. W. Norton and Co., 1939. Pp. 154.

Educational Policies Commission. *The Education of Free Men in American Democracy*. Washington: National Education Association, 1941. Pp. 115.

ERSKINE, JOHN. "Humanities in the New College Program." *Journal of Higher Education*, XVIII (May, 1947), 227–34.

EURICH, ALVIN C. "A Renewed Emphasis upon General Education." *General Education in the American College*. Thirty-eighth Yearbook of the National Society for the Study of Education, Part II. Bloomington: Public School Publishing Co., 1939. Pp. 3–14.

FLEMING, WILLIAM. "Survey of Fine Arts Course in the College of Liberal Arts at Syracuse University." *Journal of General Education*, III (October, 1948), 6–15.

FOLGER, RUTH A. "Art for the College Undergraduate." *Education,* LXIII (December, 1942), 208–12.

FOLLETT, MARY PARKER. *Dynamic Administration: The Collected Papers of Mary Parker Follett.* Edited by Henry C. Metcalf and L. Urwick. New York: Harper and Brothers, 1942. Pp. 320.

FROMM, ERICH. *Escape from Freedom.* New York: Rinehart and Co., 1941. Pp. ix + 305.

GARDNER, JANE L. "Art for the College Undergraduate." *Education,* LXIII (December, 1942), 232–34.

GIEDION, SIEGFRIED. *Mechanization Takes Command.* New York: Oxford University Press, 1948. Pp. xiv + 743.

GILL, ERIC. *Art.* London: John Lane, 1934. Pp. xi + 158.

GOLDWATER, ROBERT. "Modern Art in the College Curriculum." *College Art Journal,* I (May, 1942), 90–93.

——. *Modern Art in Your Life.* New York: Museum of Modern Art, 1949. Pp. 48.

——. "Teaching of Art in the Colleges of the United States." *College Art Journal,* Supplement II (May, 1943). Pp. 31.

GORER, GEOFFREY. *The American People.* New York: W. W. Norton and Co., 1948. Pp. 246.

GRAEFFE, ARNOLD D. *Creative Education in the Humanities.* New York: Harper and Brothers, 1951. Pp. xiv + 199.

GRIMES, JAMES. "Problems of Materials in Art Education." *Educational Research Bulletin,* XXIII (January, 1944), 20–22.

HAGGERTY, MELVIN. *Art a Way of Life.* Minneapolis: University of Minnesota Press, 1935. Pp. 43.

HAMILTON, WALTON H. "Competition." *Encyclopedia of the Social Sciences.* New York: The Macmillan Company, 1937. Pp. 141–47.

Harvard University Committee. *General Education in a Free Society.* Cambridge: Harvard University Press, 1946. Pp. xix + 267.

HIRSCH, STEFAN. "Report on Art at Bard College." *College Art Journal,* VII (Summer, 1948), 302–07.

HOLT, GEORGE. "The Bennington Program: Art as a Basic Course in the Curriculum." *College Art Journal,* VII (Spring, 1948), 172–76.

HOOK, SIDNEY. *Education for Modern Man.* New York: Dial Press, 1946. Pp. xiv + 237.

HORNEY, KAREN. *Our Inner Conflicts: A Constructive Theory of Neurosis.* New York: W. W. Norton and Co., 1945. Pp. 250.

HUTCHINS, ROBERT M. *The Higher Learning in America.* New Haven: Yale University Press, 1936. Pp. 119.

Institute of Administrative Research, Teachers College, Columbia University. *Still Unfinished: Our Educational Obligation to America's Children.* Washington: National Education Association, 1948. Pp. 33.

JONES, HOWARD MUMFORD. "Art and General Education." *College Art Journal,* VII (Spring, 1948), 157–60.

KALLEN, HORACE M. *Art and Freedom.* 2 vols. New York: Duell, Sloan, and Pearce, 1942. Pp. xvii + ix + 1006.

——. *The Education of Free Men.* New York: Farrar, Straus, and Co., 1949. Pp. xix + 332.

KILPATRICK, WILLIAM H. "Philosophy of Education from the Experimentalist Outlook." *Philosophies of Education.* Forty-first Yearbook of the National Society for the Study of Education, Part I. Chicago: The Society, 1942. Pp. 39–86.

KILPATRICK, WILLIAM H. AND OTHERS. *The Educational Frontier.* New York: D. Appleton-Century Company, 1933. Pp. vi + 325.

KRUG, EDWARD A. *Curriculum Planning.* New York: Harper and Brothers, 1950. Pp. xi + 306.

LANGER, SUSANNE K. *Philosophy in a New Key.* Cambridge: Harvard University Press, 1942. Pp. xiv + 313.

———. "The Principles of Creation in Art." *The Hudson Review,* II (Winter, 1949), 515–34.

LAPORTE, PAUL M. "The Introductory Course Again." *College Art Journal,* III (November, 1943), 20–24.

LONGMAN, LESTER D. "Contemporary Art in Historical Perspective." *College Art Journal,* VIII (Autumn, 1948), 3–8.

LYND, ROBERT S. *Knowledge for What? The Place of Social Science in American Culture.* Princeton: Princeton University Press, 1939. Pp. x + 268.

McCORKLE, T. S. "The Objectives of Education in the Fine Arts." *Association of American Colleges Bulletin,* XXXV (December, 1949), 544–55.

McGRATH, EARL J. "The Fine Arts in General Education." *Art Education Organizes.* 1949 Yearbook of the National Art Education Association. Kutztown: The Association, 1949. Pp. 37–48.

McGRATH, EARL J. AND OTHERS. *Toward General Education.* New York: The Macmillan Company, 1948. Pp. vii + 224.

MACK, R. P. "An Experimental Course in Aesthetics." *Journal of Higher Education,* XXI (April, 1950), 204–06.

MACMAHON, D. H. "A New Approach to the Humanities." *Journal of Higher Education,* XVII (November, 1946), 415–20.

MACMURRAY, JOHN. *Reason and Emotion.* New York: D. Appleton-Century Company, 1936. Pp. 278.

MATHER, FRANK JEWETT. "Old Art or New." *College Art Journal,* I (January, 1942), 31–33.

MATHEWS, CONAN. "Why Art in a College Education?" *Education,* LX (November, 1939), 165–69.

MEAD, MARGARET. "Art and Reality." *College Art Journal,* II (May, 1943), 119–21.

MEARNS, HUGHES. *The Creative Adult.* New York: Doubleday & Company, Inc., 1940. Pp. viii + 300.

MOHOLY-NAGY, L. *Vision in Motion.* Chicago: Paul Theobald, 1947. Pp. 371.

MUMFORD, LEWIS. *City Development: Studies in Disintegration and Renewal.* New York: Harcourt, Brace and Co., 1945. Pp. 248.

———. *Technics and Civilization.* New York: Harcourt, Brace and Co., 1934. Pp. xi + 495.

MURPHY, GARDNER. *Personality: A Biosocial Approach to Origins and Structure.* New York: Harper and Brothers, 1947. Pp. xii + 999.

MURRAY, H. A. *Explorations in Personality.* New York: Oxford University Press, 1938. Pp. 761.

MURSELL, JAMES L. "The Arts in American Education." *Educational Forum,* VIII (January, 1944), 151–57.

NORTHROP, F. S. C. *The Meeting of East and West.* New York: The Macmillan Company, 1946. Pp. xxii + 531.

OGDEN, ROBERT M. "Fine Arts as Humanistic Studies." *Education,* LXIII (April, 1943), 505–11.

———. *Psychology and Education.* New York: Harcourt, Brace and Co., 1932. Pp. xiv + 350.

OSBORN, ELODIE COURTER. *Texture and Pattern.* New York: Museum of Modern Art, 1949. Pp. 2 + 40 pl.

Progressive Education Association. *The Visual Arts in General Education.* New York: D. Appleton-Century Company, 1940. Pp. x + 166.

RANNELLS, EDWARD W. "Art in the Humanities." *College Art Journal,* VIII (Summer, 1949), 256–67.

READ, HERBERT. *Art and Society.* 2nd ed. New York: Pantheon Books, Inc., 1950. Pp. xv + 152.

———. *Education through Art.* New York: Pantheon Books, Inc., 1949. Pp. xxiii + 320.

———. *The Grass Roots of Art.* New York: Wittenborn, Schultz, Inc., 1949. Pp. 92.

RUSK, W. S. "Arts in Liberal Education." *College Art Journal,* I (January, 1942), 22–25.

RUSSELL, BERTRAND. *Education and the Modern World.* New York: W. W. Norton and Co., 1932. Pp. 245.

SAYERS, DOROTHY. *The Mind of the Maker.* New York: Harcourt, Brace and Co., 1941. Pp. xvi + 229.

SCHMECKEBIER, LAURENCE. "Humanities in the Modern World." *College Art Journal,* II (March, 1943), 76–80.

———. "Modern Art First, Not Last." *College Art Journal,* I (March, 1942), 60–63.

SHOEMAKER, FRANCIS. *Aesthetic Experience and the Humanities.* New York: Columbia University Press, 1943. Pp. xvii + 339.

SUPER, DONALD E. *The Dynamics of Vocational Adjustment.* New York: Harper and Brothers, 1942. Pp. xiii + 286.

The President's Commission on Higher Education. *Higher Education in American Democracy.* Vol. I, *Establishing the Goals.* New York: Harper and Brothers, 1948. Pp. 103.

U. S. Bureau of the Census. *Statistical Abstract of the United States: 1949.* Washington: U. S. Government Printing Office, 1949.

U. S. Office of Education. *Biennial Survey of Education, 1944-46.* Chapter I. Washington: U. S. Government Printing Office, 1949.

University of Minnesota. "The General College." *The Bulletin of the University of Minnesota,* LII (July 6, 1949), 20.

WASHBURN, HELEN P. "Creative Arts and Higher Education." *Association of American Colleges Bulletin,* XXX (December, 1944), 552–65; XXXI (March-October, 1945), 84–94, 268–78, 418–27.

YOUNG, J. DONALD. "Art in the Liberal Arts College: How It Has Been Taught and How It Should Be Taught." *College Art Journal,* V (November, 1945), 8–14.

ZIEGFELD, EDWIN. "The College Art Program in General Education." *Journal of General Education,* II (April, 1948), 238–45.

Index

INDEX

Adams, Phillip R., 148
Adler, Mortimer J., 47
Administration:
  and scheduling art courses, 211–12
  and teaching staff, 215–17
  of art program, 208–19
  of art workshops, 212–13
  of exhibit program, 213–14, 218–19
  of general campus activities, 212–14
  of loan collection of prints and re-
    productions, 214
  of plant and facilities, 217–19
  of required *vs.* elective courses, 208–
    11
Affective factors in esthetic response,
  68 ff.
Alberty, Harold, 201
American culture:
  divisive influences in, 21–39
  dominant trends in, 106–11
    industrial technology, 109–11
    materialism, 108–09
    scientific bias, 106–08
  effects of dominant trends in, 111–23
    high standard of living, 111
    increase in leisure time, 112–13
    interdependence and isolation,
    113–15

    loss of opportunity for creative
     activity, 115–20
    rejection of esthetic values, 120–23
  potential role of the arts in, 124–29
American Institute of Public Opinion,
  27
Art:
  achievements in, as related to total
    cultural pattern, 95–100, 183–84
  and creativity, 75–81
  and the expression of group values,
    100–05
  and human experience, 66–81
  and intercultural understanding,
    104–05
  and revelation of the self, 91–92
  as expression, 89–93, 147, 179–80,
    182 ff., 198–99
  as intensification of experience, 86–
    87, 91–92
  as propaganda, 102
  contemporary, importance of, in
    art program, 152–53, 168, 195–96
  courses, *See* Courses in art
  experience, and personal growth,
    82–93
    distinctive characteristics of, 71–75
    not always pleasurable, 88

relating art instruction to, 201–03
Student planning:
as an educational concept, 45–49
in art courses, 203–05
Studio activities:
facilities necessary for, 217–18
importance of, in art courses, 144, 146–49
in an integrated art course, 163–64
integration of, with classroom work, 172, 173, 174, 175, 186–87, 193–94
nature of, in art course, 197–201
student planning of, 204
use of college and community resources for, 206–07
Super, Donald E., 60–61
Symphonic form, influence of industrial society on, 101

Technology:
depersonalization resulting from, 116–18
in American culture, 109–11
interdependence resulting from, 113–15
specialization in, 110, 115–16
standardization in, 118–19

Understanding, common, essential for achievement of common goals, 16–17
Unity in esthetic experience, 67–68
U. S. Bureau of the Census, 24
U. S. Office of Education, 27
University of Minnesota:
General College, 143
General Arts course, 143
Humanities course, 143
Utility value:
and esthetic value, 61–72, 73–75, 87
of science, 72–74

Van Gogh, Vincent, 101
Visual materials:
facilities needed for art courses, 217
use of, in art courses, 191–92, 193–97

Washburn, Helen P., 148
Wayne University, integrated art course, 161
Workshops in art for general student body, 212–13

Ziegfeld, Edwin, 197–98